Land registration and cadastral systems

Titles of related interest

Geographical Information Systems
Principles and Applications
Edited by D J Maguire, M F Goodchild and D W Rhind

Handling Geographical Information
Methodology and Potential Applications
Edited by I Masser and M Blakemore

Map Generalization
Making Rules for Knowledge Representation
Edited by P B Buttenfield and R B McMaster

Economic Activity and Land Use
The Changing Information Base for Local and Regional Studies
Edited by M J Healey

Land registration and cadastral systems

Tools for land information and management

Gerhard Larsson

Longman
Scientific &
Technical
Copublished in the United States with
John Wiley & Sons, Inc., New York

Longman Scientific and Technical,
Longman Group UK Limited,
Longman House, Burnt Mill, Harlow,
Essex CM20 2JE, England
and Associated Companies throughout the world

Copublished in the United States with
John Wiley & Sons, Inc., 605 Third Avenue, New York, NY 10158

Trademarks
Throughout this book trademarked names are used. Rather than put a trademark symbol in every occurrence of a trademarked name, we state that we are using the names only in an editorial fashion and to the benefit of the trademark owner with no intention of infringement of the trademark.

First published 1991

British Library Cataloguing in Publication Data
Larsson, Gerhard
    Land registration and cadastral systems: Tools
    for land information and management.
    I. Title
    333.3

    ISBN 0–582–08952–2

Library of Congress Cataloging-in-Publication Data
Larsson, Gerhard, 1920–
    Land registration and cadastral systems: tools for land
    information and management / Gerhard Larsson.
        p.   cm.
    Includes bibliographical references and index.
    ISBN 0–470–21798–7
    1. Land use – Data processing.   2. Land titles – Registration and
    transfer – Data processing.   3. Cadasters – Data processing.
    4. Information storage and retrieval systems – Land use.   I. Title.
    HD108.15.L37   1991
    333.3′028′5 – dc20   91–23717
                                                              CIP

Set in 10/12pt Times

Printed and Bound in Great Britain
at the Bath Press, Avon

Contents

Preface

Problems concerning the optimal use of land resources and improved land management are important all over the world. With increasing population pressures and a greater need for environmental controls, they must be given still greater attention. It is easy to find examples of the misuse of land resources, weak or non-existent planning, poor management and insufficient land regulation. The remedies are often difficult to develop and still more difficult to implement.

However, better and more detailed knowledge about the present situation and expected developments with regard to land and water would be an important basis for further action. The problem of how to develop good land information systems (LIS) has, therefore, been debated extensively, especially since automation has greatly increased our ability to handle masses of data.

Information related to specified land units is a cornerstone of LIS, since data concerning ownership and other property rights, boundaries, areas, land uses, market and assessed values, buildings, habitation, etc., are all interrelated. The present study is devoted to the problem of developing efficient information systems based on such land units. It presents the historical background and the experiences gained from existing cadastres and land registers, discusses benefits and analyses methods, problems and alternatives — especially in countries, where such systems currently are lacking or underdeveloped. It has been proven that they can form a natural basis for comprehensive, multipurpose land information systems of great importance for improved planning, management and control.

This study does not attempt to develop entirely new models, but rather is based mainly on experience gained in different parts of the world. I have, however, tried to use my own judgement to evaluate different methods. My ambition has been to provide an overview without delving too deeply into technical matters. Those looking for detailed descriptions of survey methods or data systems are, therefore, advised to consult specialized literature in the field.

I would like to express my gratitude for all the valuable comments given to me by many different people during the course of my work on various projects in South Asia and eastern Africa, during the decades I served on the Commission of Cadastre and Rural Land Management of the International Federation of Surveyors and during my period as chairman of the United Nations Ad Hoc Group of Experts on Cadastral Surveying and Mapping. I would especially like to thank Professor J. L. G. Henssen, President of the International Office of Cadastre and Land Records, and Mr J. C. D. Lawrance, former Land Tenure Adviser in the Overseas Development Administration. Financial support for the study has been provided by the Swedish Council for Building Research. Dr Thomas Miller and Dr Jan Brzeski have kindly reviewed my English.

Gerhard Larsson
Professor of Real Estate Planning
The Royal Institute of Technology, Stockholm.

Acknowledgements

We are grateful to the following for permission to reproduce copyright material:

The Controller of Her Majesty's Stationery Office for Fig. 4.4 (Dale, 1976), and Fig. 11.1 (Simpson, 1976) published by Cambridge University Press; International Federation of Surveyors (FIG) for Figs 5.4 (Greulich 1983) & 13.4 (Chrisman *et al.*, 1986); The World Bank for Fig. 6.1 (Feder, 1986). United Nations for extracts from the *Report of the Ad Hoc Group of Experts on Cadastral Surveying* 1973, 1985 and The World Bank for extracts from Lawrence *Seminar on Land Information Systems* 1985.

Whilst every effort has been made to trace the owners of copyright material, in a few cases this has proved impossible and we take this opportunity to offer our apologies to any copyright holders whose rights we may have unwittingly infringed.

1

Land information systems – tools for development

1.1 The need for land information

There is a growing need all over the world for land information as a basis for planning, development and control of land resources. Continuing expansion of production in the industrialized world exerts increasing pressure on scarce natural resources. Similar pressures on natural resources in the Third World stem mainly from unabated population growth. Land, being in one way or another the basic source of most material wealth, is of crucial importance and will require effective management systems (Fig. 1.1).

It is easy to find examples – especially in developing countries – of what happens when the situation gets out of control. As far as agriculture is concerned, one can identify unsuitable land uses with drought, famine and serious erosion as possible consequences. Appropriate land uses may also be mismanaged because of unsuitable agrarian patterns and outdated tenure systems with inadequate protection of tenure rights. Forest lands may be exposed to excessive and uncontrolled exploitation with resultant soil conservation problems and shortages of wood fuel. The staggering land-use problems confronting urban areas are usually traced to rapid urbanization and massive urban growth in recent decades. Most new settlements in urban areas of the Third World are irregular, uncontrolled and often of slum character. Urban planning, as it is usually understood, has practically collapsed in many countries.

Consequently, there is a growing outcry for better land management and development controls by the public sector. But how can we plan and control without having sufficient knowledge and information about the basic element – the land itself? General knowledge is not enough; what is required is detailed information about land use: who owns the land, who occupies and works it, what is the pattern of land use, etc.

For this rather obvious reason, the need for land information systems (LIS)

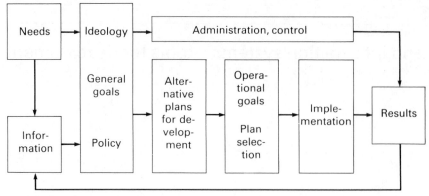

Fig. 1.1 Land management

has become an urgent problem. There is much debate about the best ways and methods to develop such systems.

1.2 The concept of LIS

Several formal definitions of LIS have been proposed. Best known is the one adopted by FIG (Féderation Internationale des Géomètres):

> A Land Information System is a tool for legal, administrative and economic decision-making and an aid for planning and development which consists on the one hand of a database containing spatially referenced land-related data for a defined area, and on the other hand, of procedures and techniques for the systematic collection, updating, processing and distribution of the data. The base of a land information system is a uniform spatial referencing system for the data in the system, which also facilitates the linking of data within the system with other land-related data.

This definition may be illustrated as in Fig 1.2.

There are, however, still differences of opinion as to the most suitable definition of LIS. According to Hamilton and Williamson (1984), one factor which creates confusion is the relationship between LIS and systems for geographical, cartographic, resource, environmental and socio-economic information. The FIG definition includes spatially referenced, land-related data from all these information systems under the LIS umbrella, while others claim that geographical information system is the generic term. This latter opinion is expressed in Fig. 1.3.

It is not within the scope of this study to discuss the definition of LIS in any depth. We can only observe that the concept of LIS is still evolving, and that there are different opinions about its relationship to geographical information systems and similar concepts. It is more important to establish the fact that there is a need for the systematic collection, updating, processing and distri-

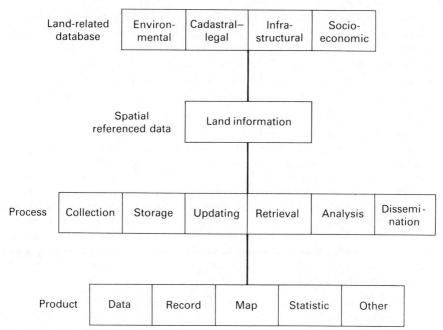

Fig. 1.2 A land information system

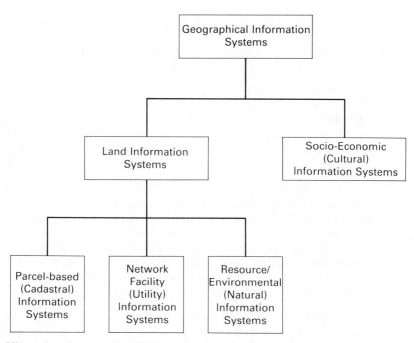

Fig. 1.3 Hierarchy of geographical information systems (from Williamson 1986)

bution of spatially referenced land related data to support legal, administrative and economic decision-making, for development planning and for evaluating the consequences of different action alternatives.

New technology – especially computerization – has greatly increased the potential for developing such systems, but has also imposed some restrictions and conditions. Weir (1984) describes the situation in the following way:

> Land related information becomes increasingly important to the orderly, fair and intelligent use and development of the land. In the past, land-related information was gathered, stored, updated and distributed on a manual basis in registers, books, plans and maps. With modern technology, these activities are now being computerized and automated throughout the world. This transition to computers is receiving major attention by private, industrial and governmental agencies all over the world. The variety of systems is great and includes fiscal systems, legal land registration systems, development control systems, facilities management systems, utility network systems, urban and rural planning information systems, land resources systems, demographic and social data systems, and the basic geographic or coordinate systems. Of primary importance in building effective, efficient, and compatible land information systems are:
>
> – the existence of an easily accessible common reference framework;
> – constructive actions by government in coordinating existing land-related functions;
> – the standardization of procedures and terminology.

1.3 The need for co-ordination: structure

As mentioned earlier, interest in computer-based systems is great, and so is the variety of systems. This means that in the near future a great many new private, local and governmental systems will be established. Without specific co-ordinating activities, these systems will only be compatible and linked to one another to a limited degree. They will cater primarily for internal information needs within individual agencies, and it will not be possible to combine them to form general information systems. It will be difficult to rectify this later on. Morgan (1985) describes the current situation within the land information field:

> The growing difficulties of planning and managing land resource development have led to a common perception that current approaches to the measurement, storage and dissemination of land data are largely inadequate. Traditional strategies have favored the establishment of independent local, regional and national authorities administering data development, acquisition and storage programs. Clearly, such approaches are myopic. The results have been programs and activities which are redundant, inflexible and occasionally counter-productive.

There is thus a real and immediate danger that information production will be specific for limited sectors, and that only limited use will be made of the latent possibilities to co-ordinate and combine different sources of information. The risk of duplication is also great. To avoid this, it is essential, as Weir has stressed, to establish easily accessible, common reference frameworks. In land information systems this means, among other things, having spatial reference systems – expressed in co-ordinates or in other ways. It also means working with common, uniquely identified units to which information can be linked – large-scale units such as land parcels, medium-scale or small-scale ones such as divisions into administrative, statistical, type and regional areas. Without this, data compiled from different sources will be more or less incompatible.

Weir also stresses the need for constructive action by *the government* to co-ordinate land information systems. The natural behaviour of a governmental department is to work more or less independently within its field of responsibility, and this also applies to information. Co-ordination and integration do not come automatically, but require continuous action.

These efforts should not be limited to the framework and technical shape of the systems. The government must also determine their functions: which department ought to be responsible for certain types of information and for certain databases; how the exchange of information among different departments should be organized; and how can information best be made available for planning and management. Governmental support and action are also necessary with regard to standardization of procedures and terminology.

Integration aspects must be studied most thoroughly. The sheer mass of land data and the need for different kinds of information are so great that they can never be covered by one or a few databases. Furthermore, the system must be constructed in steps and be flexible enough to permit the successive addition of new kinds of data. The system can thus develop gradually to satisfy an increasing array of needs.

A natural way to organize the data management is the 'nodal' approach (see Sedunary 1984). It is characterized by the establishment of major databases as primary nodes within the LIS framework, thus centralizing systems with strong interrelationships. These primary nodes act as communications hubs for secondary, dependent systems serving individual applications and located on comparatively minor, peripheral databases. This approach is diagrammatically portrayed in Fig. 1.4. For example, the legal/fiscal node can integrate databases with functions having to do primarily with property description, title registration, valuation and land tax. Later on other functions might be added. The system thus provides flexibility and makes possible future development, while the nodal organization gives it a logical and functional structure. In most cases the development and maintenance of the primary nodes is a governmental responsibility. Many departments and agencies are normally involved, as it is still advantageous to let the most competent agency manage data collection and data retrieval within its own area. But co-ordination is necessary for integration and establishment of the overall structure.

The secondary databases on the other hand may well be developed by local or private organizations. They can be based partly on data from the primary

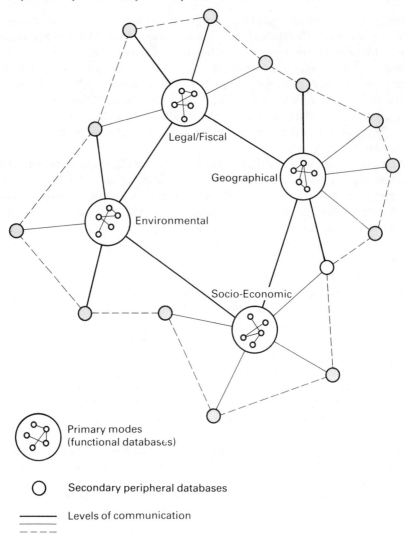

Legal/Fiscal

Geographical

Environmental

Socio-Economic

Primary modes
(functional databases)

○ Secondary peripheral databases

—— Levels of communication

Fig. 1.4 Nodal approach to a land database configuration (from Sedunary 1984)

bases and partly on additional data which are collected by the organization for its own purpose. The secondary bases can thus be designed to suit a special organization, but they are still constructed within the same general frame-work, and use the same, uniquely defined units as building blocks. This is the main difference between the nodal approach and the alternative of a number of isolated databases. The latter generally leads to excessive duplication and limited external use of the information collected.

The nodal arrangement can also make possible an appropriate balance between centralized and decentralized elements in the system. Up to now systems have often been centralized in character, and relied to a great extent on mainframe computers. Such systems were often efficient but not very user friendly, as they are difficult to adapt to the needs of the individual user. The new developments make it possible to combine centralized primary bases with secondary bases adapted to the wants of the individual user, while still affording abundant opportunity for intercommunication.

The discussion above presupposes that the information systems are computerized. This is still not always the case, especially in developing countries, but this is mainly a matter of time. In the long run most basic information will be handled by computers. Long-term planning should recognize this by organizing manual records in such a way as to facilitate computerization and integration into comprehensive systems.

So let us suppose that in the future, data will be organized into natural groups – such as primary nodes – centralizing systems having strong interrelationships. One very important group will then certainly be systems based on uniquely defined, small and homogeneous parcels of land units – *provided that a comprehensive parcel system has been established*.

1.4 Parcel-based LIS

We shall discuss later the concept of a parcel in more depth. Here, we can use the term to express a unit of land with homogeneous tenure interests.

Why, then, are parcel-based land information systems of such importance?

A primary reason is that much of human life, human activities and human property have meaningful links with specific pieces of land (Fig 1.5). This is

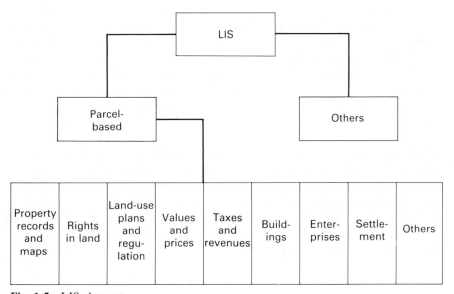

Fig. 1.5 LIS elements

obviously true in the case of rights to land – ownership, occupancy, lease, mortgage, etc. These are central to the whole sphere of economic life, since – not least in developing countries – land is the main resource for economic activities. The question of who disposes of the land and has rights in the land is, therefore, of vital importance. There are other connections as well. For instance, the most natural way to determine and locate a population is by reference to its dwelling sites which can be defined through the parcel numbers. Enterprises can be located in the same way. Taxes are largely dependent on landed property, and tax registers are, therefore, often based on land units. The same is true of establishments of different kinds such as buildings, etc. It is, therefore, natural to tie together data referring to land, buildings, people, enterprises, property, taxes, building regulations, etc., in an integrated system. Such a system must have one or more identification keys that trace all data back to a common basis. One such key is the numbered and defined piece of land.

A further addition to the information normally contained in a record of parcels can greatly increase its scope and usefulness. Parcel numbers do not express the geographical location of a property directly. This has led to the idea of *geocodes*. These are normally the co-ordinates of boundary points or of a certain point on the parcel such as the centroid or the principal building, if any. Geocodes permit a direct relationship between the information and its geographical location. In this way all information stored in the data system in question can be automatically transcribed on to maps. The information is no longer tied to a certain administrative area, but can be included in any selected and delimited area. Parcel-based information systems, therefore, have great flexibility.

We will now leave the general issues concerning LIS even though they will still constitute a background to the problems discussed. Instead we will concentrate on the basic elements of a parcel-based system: the unique identification of the land units by their indications, extent and boundaries, and the establishment of cadastre/land registers for determining fiscal obligations, ownership and other rights. The fiscal–legal part of the parcel-based system is the determinant for its whole structure. It is a long-term and costly investment, which must be considered and discussed very carefully before decisions are taken. How can an efficient system be established and maintained with limited resources?

When dealing with this problem, much can, of course, be learned from earlier experiences. After defining some concepts, we shall, therefore, discuss developments and experiences from the industrialized countries. But the question posed above is most relevant in countries which do not yet have any comprehensive, efficient system of cadastre/land registration. This is most often the case in developing countries. The discussion will, therefore, give special consideration to them.

2

General aspects of land delimitation and documentation. Cadastre and land registration

2.1 Property rights and land delimitation

Historically, the need for delimitation arose as soon as anyone – a tribe, a family, or an individual – laid claim to a particular right in an area. Hunting, fishing and grazing rights were often rather vaguely demarcated, while cultivation rights tended to have more carefully defined limits. These limits could be determined in different ways: by occupation, by fights among competing groups, by mutual agreement or by applying the customary rules.

In sparsely populated areas, the process of establishing definite boundaries began rather recently. When Africa was colonized, for example, there was still much land not effectively claimed by any family or tribe, which could therefore be treated as crown land and perhaps later given to European settlers. On the American continent and in remoter parts of Europe such as northern Sweden, the demarcation process was not finished until late in the nineteenth century.

Delimitation is thus closely linked to the development of property rights. Real-property rights can be seen not only as a means of securing exclusive control of resources within a given area, but also as a method of protecting resources or investments. If hunting or grazing in an area is open to everyone, there will be a risk of overhunting or overgrazing. Restricting such activities is, therefore, the owner's first step; he might follow this up with constructive measures – improving the hunting or fishing conditions, facilitating grazing by digging wells, etc. Such measures will seldom be undertaken if the owner himself does not retain the right to enjoy the fruits of his activities. In this sense the establishment of real-property rights is an effective means of stimulating the development of land.

In the early stages of a civilization, such rights may appropriately belong to a collective body – the tribe, group or extended family. Hunting, fishing and grazing can advantageously be undertaken by a group within a common area.

Among other advantages, this collective use reduces supervision and demarcation costs such as fencing. However, when people settle and start to cultivate the land, the situation changes. Normally the cultivator will be recognized as having an individual right, often only the right of usufruct, in the cultivated area.

There is, however, a tendency for the continued use of land to lead to stronger individual rights. This usufructuary title is often passed on from generation to generation, and is eventually often converted to individual ownership – with the right to retain the land even without cultivating it, and the right to sell the land outside the group. This process has more or less run its course in most countries, but it can still be studied in some parts of the world, e.g. in the Pacific region and in Africa south of Sahara. It is very likely that this trend towards individual, long-term, usufructuary title approaching outright ownership will continue in the future. One influence which promoted this trend was early colonial statutory law. But perhaps more important for the future is the fact that intensified cultivation requires secure land rights, both to protect investments and to secure bank loans for further investment. It is also obvious that with a rapidly growing population, competition for land will increase and there will be still more incentive to protect individual rights.

With intensified use and stronger family or individual rights, it becomes necessary to define and delimit the areas concerned both for social and economic reasons. Economists such as Demsetz (1967) tend to stress the economic factors. New property rights emerge in response to adjustments to new benefit–cost relationships, to changes in technology and relative prices, etc. New rights often require new delimitations. To subdivide an area of common use into units for individual use causes inconvenience and expense. On the other hand, communal rights do not permit the user to exclude other members of the group from enjoying the possible fruits of his own efforts. Mutual agreements may solve the problem, but negotiation costs are often too high to allow an optimal solution. As land use intensifies, these disadvantages gradually reach a point where a change in the system of property rights – property definition and demarcation becomes necessary.

In Fig. 2.1 this kind of reasoning is exemplified by illustrating the benefits (*b*) and costs (*c*) of three different systems 1–3 of land definition/demarcation. Even at a low intensity (*i*), it may be economically justifiable to establish a simple and basic system of property rights/demarcation such as village ownership and village demarcation by simple landmarks. If the intensity and/or the benefit level increases (stage 2), it may be economically feasible to change to a more advanced system, such as individual ownership or long-term occupancy combined with fences, stones, etc., for individual boundary demarcation. As land use becomes still more intensive and commercialized, the need for security, credit, public management, etc., make economically feasible the documentation and definition of individual ownership and boundaries by land records and maps (stage 3). Seen from a purely economic viewpoint, the combined system of property rights and definition/ demarcation of property units will then develop to the point where the difference between benefits and costs is greatest, that is at a certain intensity stage system 1 will turn into 2. If the intensity (taken in a wide sense as an expression for development) increases still further system 2 will turn into system 3.

In practice, economic factors alone do not determine the choice of system. Factors such as tradition and ideology naturally come into play and, in fact, the whole socio-economic environment, not just the intensity of land use, is decisive. The stages mentioned above are only examples; other combinations are possible. If the costs are kept low, it may be economically feasible to use land records and boundary maps even at the level of common ownership. If Fig. 2.1 gives only a rough illustration of the relationships, it does show that systems of property rights are related to the definition and delimitation of these rights on the ground and in maps and records, and further that these systems should be adapted to the intensity of land use and to land values. It is also likely that more advanced systems will come into use as more intense land use and commercialization lead to higher land values and increased competition for land. These are factors which promote private property rights as well as improved documentation of rights and land units. The question of land recording systems will, therefore, become increasingly significant in developing countries.

In our discussion above we have made the assumption that the development of land property rights not only necessitated demarcation on the ground, but also sooner or later necessitated further definition of the land units in maps and records. As this assumption may not be self-evident, we shall now present some brief arguments in favour of such official documentation. Later on – especially in Chapters 6 and 7 – this theme will be further developed.

2.2   Justification for land documentation

Individuals with land rights and society as a whole derive a number of benefits from the large-scale documentation of land units – in maps, records, and so on. Although most of the advantages are beneficial to both private and public interests, it may nevertheless be useful to discuss the benefits according to their particular importance for each of the two sectors.

From the viewpoint of the *private* sector, a unique definition of land units in maps and records has the following particular benefits:

• It greatly facilitates all transactions concerning land, and makes such transactions easier, cheaper and more secure. Because private conveyance of unregistered land units is often expensive, one consequence of the documentation of land units is the stimulation of the land market.

• It provides security and protection for the owner as well as for others with land rights. This security stimulates investment and development, particu-

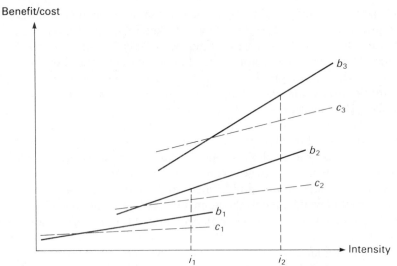

Fig. 2.1 Benefits, costs and turnover points for three different systems of property rights/property delimitation

larly through long-term credits secured by land. Most banking institutions insist on plans and a sound title before granting loans or mortgages.

- It greatly reduces disputes and litigation over land, resulting in better social and human relationships, less work for the courts, and less expense for the individual. Especially in the developing countries, much of the work of the courts is concerned with disputes about land. As a rule, it is harder for a poor man to defend his interests than for a big landowner.

From a *public* viewpoint the following benefits are of special importance:

- For many purposes information based on comparatively small land units, such as ownership units, can be an important part of more complex *land information systems*. By the middle of the 1950s the Swedish geographer Hägerstrand had already pointed out the advantages of basing such systems on this unit rather than on more artificial divisions, such as grid systems, etc. The main argument in favour of using property units as building blocks is their importance for economic decision-making and new development. Such units are effective sources of information about ownership and other property rights, about credit, taxation, assessed valuation, etc. They can also be used in conjunction with many other types of information, such as population data. If the land units are related to a general spatial reference system, all this information can then be positioned geographically.

In many countries such accurate information is important as a means of increasing public revenue by fair land taxation.

- It permits *better land use and management*. As land is a basic resource for every community and country, this advantage is a very important one. Better land use can be encouraged through planning and development regulations. Such improved land use can occur through direct action, such as public urban development, land consolidation, irrigation projects, etc. But it can also be achieved by providing good conditions for private development, such as secure ownership, access to bank loans, etc., that is those advantages discussed above under private benefits. Land records based on well-defined land units are essential for all these purposes. The same can be said about efficient land management. It is self-evident that thorough knowledge of ownership, land units, and boundaries will contribute greatly to effective land management.

- *Public control and land-policy measures* also require land records of defined units. Such measures include the implementation of plans and other guidelines for development and land use, agrarian reforms, control of excessive fragmentation, control of foreign ownership, etc. These measures are difficult without a system for recording transfers, ownership, land boundaries, and land use.

2.3 The unit of record

For all of the purposes mentioned above, a system of uniquely-defined land units, which cannot be changed except through legal process, is imperative. If the units can be changed informally, information given in different land records would soon become inaccurate and misleading. The basis for land credit and secure land rights is weakened if there is no guarantee that the records are in complete agreement with the actual boundaries and units. Similarly, the ability of local governments to direct development and implement and control land policy is lessened if land can be transferred between units and units can be subdivided by private agreements without public consent and recording. To maintain a system of legally determined units is not only in the private interest but also strongly in the public interest. It is, therefore, only reasonable that the effort and expense of establishing and maintaining such a system are to a great extent borne by the public sector.

What principles should be followed in selecting a legal land unit that would be most suitable as a basis for all primary land records?

The unit can be chosen from many different levels (see Fig. 2.2). Three points deserve emphasis:

1. The unit should be able to serve such important private functions as

economic decision-making and development, transfers, mortgages, long-term use agreements, etc. It should, therefore, be closely related to existing property rights. All legal or other changes which weaken this connection may diminish the usefulness of the system.

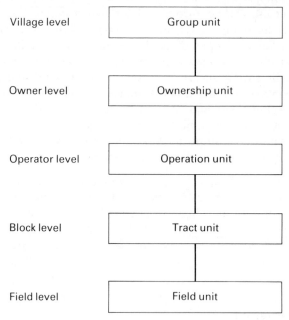

Village level	Group unit
Owner level	Ownership unit
Operator level	Operation unit
Block level	Tract unit
Field level	Field unit

Fig.2.2   Different land unit levels

2. The unit should be able to serve important public functions: to provide data for an information base and for the collection of taxes and other public revenues, land control, etc. These needs correspond largely to the needs of the private sector, as both depend heavily on property rights.

3. The units should be relatively stable. As all unit changes must be officially documented, too many changes result in increased costs for maintaining the system. Therefore, for example, a unit determined according to short-term leasing arrangements is not suitable.

Looking at actual practice, we find that in some countries the landholding as a whole – determined by ownership or occupancy – is chosen as the basic unit for land records. As is well known, however, a landholding or a farm may often consist of several different blocks of land, sometimes located far away from each other. Many countries, therefore, prefer using continuous blocks as units of record.

Simpson (1976, p. 4) discusses this problem in the following way:

> The purpose for which land registration is required is of great importance, for it should determine the choice of the record unit. If the purpose is fiscal, value will be

the principal objective and the most suitable unit of record may be the *unit of use*; for example, in agricultural property the units of use are the individual fields which vary in size and quality and so in value. The fields together make up the farm or *unit of operation*, an appropriate unit where development is concerned or the implementation of laws regulating land use. Two or more units of operation – whether contiguous or not – may, however, form a *unit of ownership*, and this appears to be the obvious unit if the purpose of the record is to keep particulars of ownership and not those of the use value.

This discussion does not, however, take into account the fact that modern land information systems are intended to serve many purposes, and that it is a great advantage to have different land records, designed for different purposes, but using common land units, which can integrate component records into one land information system. The choice of the land unit should, therefore, take these requirements into consideration.

One solution used by several countries in continental Europe is to use the continuous tract of land – the *parcel* – as the basic unit for land records. If required, several parcels can then be combined to form larger units as units of operation or ownership.

Henssen and McLaughlin (1986, p. 8) define cadastral parcel as follows: 'A cadastral parcel is a continuous tract of land within which unique tenure interests are recognized. The cadastral parcel must envelop a continuous area of land and a continuous interest in land. On the map a cadastral parcel is formed by a, in itself closed, line which encloses the map, and has a unique identification.'

The UN Ad Hoc Group of Experts on Cadastral Surveying and Land Information Systems (1985) used the following definition: 'For the cadastre the basic spatial unit is known as the parcel. A *land parcel*, known in some countries as a *lot*, *plot* or even a *plat*, is an area of land whose separate identity may be defined by the limit of legal rights, by responsibility for taxation payments or by use.' In this definition it is not explicitly stated that the basic spatial unit should be a continuous tract. As mentioned, in several countries this unit is rather the original farm and may consist of several tracts.

For convenience, we shall use the word 'parcel' more or less as a synonym for the primary land unit, whether or not this unit consists of one continuous tract. Larger units will be called sections, blocks, etc. In common practice the parcel designation consists of a name or number of the section/block and a unique number within it for the parcel in question. When the unit is changed – for example by subdivision – different practices are followed. Most commonly, the new/changed units are assigned new numbers or sub-numbers of the original number.

2.4 Cadastres and legal land registers

Historically, land records have been established to serve two main purposes. First, as 'fiscal' records, primarily for the public sector, they have served as the basis for the full and accurate taxation of land. Second, as 'legal' records, primarily for the private sector, they have served as registers of ownership and other land rights.

On the European continent the development of fiscal/taxation record systems was heavily influenced by the decision of Napoleon I to establish a French *cadastre*. The original meaning of this word is somewhat obscure. To cite Simpson (1976, p. 4): 'The derivation of the word "cadastre" used to be ascribed to the Latin *capitastrum* which was taken to be a contraction of *capitum registrum*, a register of *capita*, literally "heads" and so by extension "taxable land units"; but modern dictionaries derive "cadastre" from the Greek word "katastikhon", meaning literally "line by line" and so a tax register.'

In continental Europe the word 'cadastre' came to mean 'a systematic classification and valuation of land, under the control of the central government, by means of maps of parcels drafted on the basis of topographical surveys and recorded according to parcels in a register' (Henssen 1971).

'Cadastre' thus had a distinct meaning as a specific type of land record – supported by maps – which included not only the area and the land use for each parcel, but also land value and ownership information. Recently, however, there has been a tendency to give the word a broader meaning, so that it is now acceptable to use the term even to refer to land records which do not include information on land values and ownership. The UN Ad Hoc Group of Experts on Cadastral Surveying and Land Information Systems (1985), uses the following definition (closely following an earlier proposal by Henssen): 'The *Cadastre* is a methodically arranged public inventory of data on the properties within a certain country or district based on a survey of their boundaries; such properties are systematically identified by means of some separate designation. The outlines of the property and the parcel identifier are normally shown on large-scale maps.' This definition is an extension of the original meaning of cadastre, but is still appropriate for current use in a period characterized by diverse types of land information systems established for more than just one purpose.

Essentially, *a cadastre is thus a systematic description of the land units within an area*. The description is made by maps that identify the location and boundaries of every unit, and by records. In the records, the most essential information is the identification number and the area of the unit, usually differentiated by land use class. Information is often provided on the unit's registration date with reference to a particular file. Furthermore, the classical cadastre provides information concerning owners, land classes and values or land taxes. Additional information may sometimes be found in the cadastral records or in adjacent records. Databases are often established for buildings, physical plans, etc., especially in automated cadastres. Sometimes such an extended cadastre will be referred to as *a multipurpose cadastre*. Strictly speaking, however, every cadastre nowadays – even in its simplest form and lacking any additional information – is multipurpose, as shown in Section 2.2.

Closely connected to the word cadastre is the term *cadastral survey*, which is simply defined as a survey of boundaries of land units. A cadastral survey may be carried out both for the initial formation of the parcel as well as for any subsequent changes of the boundaries. A cadastral survey may also be conducted in order to re-establish missing boundaries.

We now come to the second type of land records, the 'legal' records, which do not serve the purposes of land taxation or the description of land units, but are intended to include the description and the determination of rights to and encumbrances on the land. It seems inappropriate to call such 'legal' records cadastres. The Germans would not call their 'Grundbuch' a cadastre, nor would the French call the records kept in their 'Bureau des Hypothèques' a cadastre. In English-speaking countries the word *cadastre* was not used until recently (except in combinations such as cadastral survey) because the land records there are mainly of the 'legal' type.

It has been suggested that such records be called 'legal cadastres'. However, we prefer to use the term '(legal) land register'. This term has long been used in English-speaking countries to describe the legal registration of rights and deeds concerning real property (as, for example, in the standard work by Simpson 1976: *Land Law and Registration*).

The legal status of a land register is closely linked to the manner in which a transaction is confirmed and documented (see Fig. 2.3).

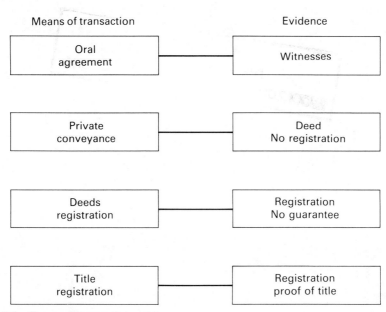

Fig. 2.3   Types of transaction evidence

We will use the following definition:

(Legal) land register is a public register of deeds and rights concerning real property. Depending on the legal system, there may be a register of deeds or a register of titles. Under the system based on the *registration of deeds*, it is the deed

itself which is registered. A *deed* is a record of a particular transaction and serves as evidence of this specific agreement, but it is not itself a proof of the legal right of the transacting parties to enter into and consummate the agreement. Under the alternative system based on a *registration of titles*, this process of tracing the chain of deeds is unnecessary. Title registration is itself a proof of ownership and its correctness is usually guaranteed and insured by the State.

(UN Ad Hoc Group of Experts on Cadastral Surveying and Mapping, 1973).

Even though there is a conceptual difference between the cadastre and the (legal) land register, it must be admitted that in practice a clear distinction is not always evident. There is, however, still a distinctive difference in essence, purpose, and focus between the two types of registers. These differences are also reflected in the organizational structures of the cadastre and land register systems. In most countries land registration is carried out by the courts or by special land registry units, while the cadastre is the responsibility of separate organizations.

3

Historical development of structure and function of cadastral and land registration systems

3.1 Early development

As mentioned earlier, there were initially two basic reasons for records regarding land: the need for the private vendee of land to get publicity for his acquisition of land and the need for the state to know all land units liable for taxation or other services, dues and fees.

Even at an early stage of development the need for some publicity regarding land transfer is evident. Land cannot be literally handed over. An agreement itself will not preclude an owner from selling the same land to two different buyers. There were also kinship rights vested in land. Therefore, it had to be officially known and proclaimed that there were no known hindrances to the transfer of ownership rights in the land. Already in the Bible do we read about the prophet Jeremiah, who had been involved in land acquisition:

> I bought the field from my cousin Hanamel of Anathot and paid him the price: seventeen silver shekels. I drew up the deed and sealed it, called in witnesses and weighted out the money on the scales. I then took both the sealed deed of purchase and its open copy in accordance with the requirements of the law and handed over the deed of purchase to Baruch. (Jer. 32:9)

Similar proceedings are found in Assyrian–Babylonian and Egyptian sources. There had to be publicity; the transfer had to take place in the presence of witnesses in order to gain validity. In ancient Nordic laws there were rules requiring that land transaction be announced at a popular court and confirmed by 12 witnesses. Similar rules could be found in many other European countries. In primitive tribes land transfers had to take place in the presence of the chief and the elders.

Later on, it became normal practice in more developed countries to deposit and officially register the deed at the court or with a notary public. Even though the procedure did not provide security of tenure to the owner, it could prevent double selling or, in the event of double selling, the priority of claims could easily be established. The only identification of the sold land was a verbal description in the deed.

There are also early evidences of land documentation for taxation and other contributions to the state. Already in ancient Egypt – as early as about 3000 BC – there is a mention of such records kept in the royal registry. The records were partly based on surveys of land. Pictures of land surveyors at work are found in some ancient tombs (see Fig. 3.1).

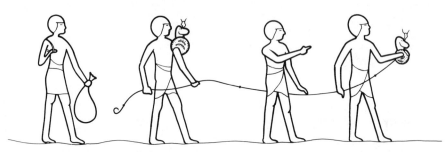

Fig. 3.1 Egyptian surveyors at work

In a strongly centralized country like Egypt it was of vital importance for the rulers to keep track of landholdings and claims on the land. For the same reason the Romans surveyed the territories they occupied. It was particularly Emperor Diocletianus who ordered, at the end of the third century AD, extensive surveys and recording for taxation purposes. It has been found probable that even in China, around 700 AD, a taxation system existed based on crop yields and supported by land survey records. In South India, around 1000 AD, Raja the Great, who founded the Chola Empire, ordered a revenue survey which was continued later by his successor.

Some decades later a famous land record – the Domesday Book – was established in England. The survey was ordered by William the Conqueror almost 20 years after he had defeated the Saxons at the battle of Hastings. It was completed in a short time in 1086. The records covered in principle the whole of England. They showed names of landowners, acreage, tenures as well as arable, meadow, pasture and forest land uses, number of tenants and quantity and type of livestock. The records were not supported by any maps.

Several types of ancient surveys (see Fig. 3.2) and records can be found in other countries. These are mostly taxation records without pertinent maps. In Sweden, for example, King Gustav I ordered in 1540 a survey of all taxable farms. The records included names of villages and farms, their owners and their tax 'strength' relative to the 'normal' farm. The records were revised and updated from time to time and trials were made later on to include some form of land surveying. The main initial task of the Swedish Land Survey, established in the early seventeenth century, was to make maps for taxation

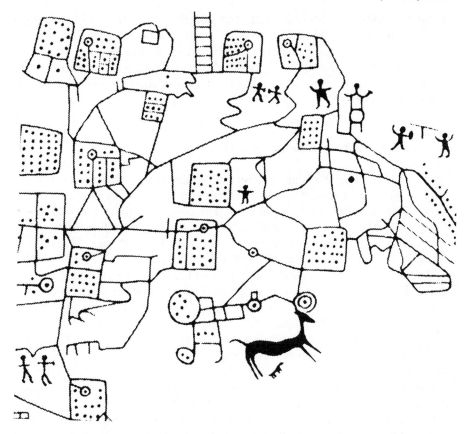

Fig. 3.2   About 1600–1400 BC, this plan of 4 m length was engraved with bronze tools on the surface of a flat rock in north Italy. Rivulets, irrigation channels and roadways are delineated as lines. A circle with a point signifies a well and a rectangular piece of ground with regular rows of points is supposed to be a cultivated field

purposes recording not only mere acreage numbers but also land productivity.

In continental Europe, several attempts were made to enhance the quality of taxation by adding map information. Examples are tax mappings in parts of northern Italy in the early eighteenth century and in the Austro-Hungarian Empire in the late eighteenth century. The real breakthrough came only with Napoleon I who instituted the French cadastre in 1807. The cadastral records were to contain parcel numbers, area, land use and land values for each owner, and they would be based on cadastral surveying which was to proceed systematically parish by parish.

Partly due to the dominating position France held during that time, the French cadastre became the model for similar efforts in other European countries. During the nineteenth century most of the countries in continental

Europe established systematic cadastral systems, although of widely varying quality and extent. The Anglo-Saxon world did not develop the French cadastre model and the word itself became hardly known there.

We will discuss the cadastral and non-cadastral development separately and begin by considering the evolution of land registration systems in the non-cadastral countries.

3.2 Development in the non-cadastral countries

In those countries the main reason for establishing land records was the private need to provide a system for secure and more efficient transfers and protection of ownership rights in land. The basic premise of the system was the earlier-mentioned principle of publicity. The early primitive models were in most countries successively replaced by the system of the deed of conveyance deposited at the court or with a notary public.

The registration of deeds was initially optional and was used rather sporadically. The depository institution functioned merely as an agent and was by no means obliged to investigate the correctness of the documents and pertinent claims. The description of the land was provided by the parties to the deed. The lack of official survey and uniform system for identification of property made such land descriptions very vague and ambiguous. Having no uniform identification system it was not possible to open a special file or entry for the land units concerned. Registration was arranged according to deposition dates rather than land units. The lack of compulsory registration, coupled with the lack of uniform identification and description, as well as the lack of entries for every unit, made it difficult to search the register to establish if the seller had in fact a secure title in the land he sold.

Such a system could only be enhanced by establishing compulsory registration. Many countries did just that regarding their deed registration systems. The main reason for this was the tax collection concern – particularly the stamp duties on transfers. These rules were not always sufficiently effective as there were often limited powers to implement the law and control its observance.

Another way to enhance the above system was to require, prior to registration, unambiguous identification of the subject land unit, preferably on the map and with a unique number, as well as title investigation. Every land unit had to be given a special file or entry where all future transactions regarding it could be recorded. If such rules were coupled with a law requiring that only the registered deeds would be protected against the third party, it led to effective replacement of the deed system with the title registration system. There was no more searching of earlier deeds to establish the seller's title. The actual status of titles was shown in the register. If, additionally, the state not only guaranteed the content of the register but also undertook to indemnify for losses on frauds and mistakes in the register, the system of land registration became very reliable indeed.

The above described system has the main features of the famous system of title registration, which was established in 1858 in South Australia following the proposal by Sir Robert Torrens. The 'Torrens system' had a great influence on the development of land registration in many countries. There may still be some deficiencies in such a system, however. In Australia, for example, a land unit was normally included in the registration system when a new land grant was given by the state. There was no automatic routine, however, for bringing into the register old grants made prior to the establishment of the register. More than a century after the title registration system was introduced in Australia, many estates were still traded according to the old rules and never showed up in the land register. And even though the registered land units were surveyed at registration time and received unique identification, they were not connected to a general reference system with a dense net of control points.

The next step, therefore, was to make the title register systematic, by bringing all the unregistered titles into the register and thus making it complete. The sporadic compilation was replaced by a systematic compulsory process. A further step was to construct a register with index maps giving a complete picture of all land units within an area. For this purpose the use could be made of the earlier sporadic surveys as well as aerial pictures, ground controls, additional/supplementary surveys, etc.

In summary, we can talk about at least four distinctive stages in the development of land registration system in the non-cadastral countries:

1. Sporadic voluntary deed registration. Mainly verbal identification and no rules on formal survey. As-it-comes current registration and no specific files/entries for each land unit.

2. Same as the above, but with compulsory registration of *deeds*.

3. Sporadic compulsory registration of *titles*. Under certain conditions – such as formation of new land units, the transfer of an existing unit, etc. – the land *must* be brought into the register, surveyed if not identifiable otherwise and the legal right of the transacting parties investigated. From then on, every new transaction concerning the land must be recorded. The register is normally guaranteed and insured by the state.

4. Systematic compulsory registration of titles. *All* land units within a proclaimed area must be brought into the register and properly identified. A further step may be to establish a register index map showing all the land units within the area.

When stage 3 prevails, two types of registration legislation will normally exist: one regarding the *old system* (deed registry) for those land units not brought into the title register, and the other regarding the *new system* (title registry). This may also be true of stage 4, but only in the districts where the systematic registration is not yet completed. After the completion, the title registry law takes over entirely.

There are certainly many intermediate stages found in various countries. South Africa, for example, has a formal registration of deeds, but in practice there is registration of titles. There is a great variety among countries with regard to quality and extent of their systems, even though all belong to the same conceptual framework presented above.

3.3 Development in the cadastral countries

Let us now turn to the countries which have some sort of cadastral system. Can we even here distinguish several development stages ? What sort of interrelationship exists between cadastre and land register ? We will try to find answers to these two questions.

The purpose of the French cadastre according to the directives given by Napoleon I were:

> To survey . . . more than 100 million parcels, to classify these parcels by the fertility of the soil, and to evaluate the production capacity of each one; to bring together under the name of each owner a list of the separate parcels which he owns; to determine on the basis of their total productive capacity, their total revenue and to make of this assessment a record which should thereafter serve as the basis of future assessment . . . (Dreux 1933)

The most spectacular in this work was the survey, which was based on control points determined by triangulation. It was undertaken systematically, area by area, normally, however, without any demarcation of the boundaries. The parcels were numbered within each section on a plan with a scale of 1:2500 or 1:1250. Thus, a unique identification was achieved for all land in the country. As the purpose was purely fiscal, it was natural to record the parcels according to owners.

The French national cadastre was completed in 1850. Its utility diminished quickly, however, due mainly to lack of updating the records and cadastral plans. The French example spread around Europe. In most of the German states, in the Netherlands and in Denmark, the cadastral surveys were completed fairly soon after the French precedence. In other Mediterranean countries, in the Balkans, and in Eastern Europe the cadastral process did not go so smoothly and it is not yet completed. The typical problems hampering the process relate not so much to the establishment of the system through compilation of records, but to its subsequent maintenance and updating of registers. A system soon loses its value if the records and maps are not continually revised.

Initially, the introduction of the cadastre did not influence the existing (legal) land registration systems to any significant degree. In the cadastral countries the two systems existed parallel to each other. However, as the cadastral system grew in extent and completeness as well as in terms of sophistication of survey and cadastral administration, it became increasingly desirable to use this unique description of land units also in the legal land registers. Already Napoleon I visualized this linkage between the cadastre and the legal land registry. He stated that:

> A good cadastre will be the best complement of my civil law code to achieve systematic order in the area of real estate property. The plans must be so developed and be made so exact that they will permit at any time to define and record the boundaries of land property limits and to prevent the confusion or law suits otherwise arising.

And from the island of St Helena he wrote in 1816:

> The cadastre just by itself could have been regarded as the real beginning of the Empire, for it meant a secure guarantee of land ownership, providing for every citizen certainty of independence.

Fairly soon the linkage between the cadastre and the (legal) land registration arose in many countries induced primarily by the unique property identification offered in the cadastre, and secondarily by the fact that the cadastre could be used as evidence of ownership. Quoting S. R. Simpson (1976, p. 122) we read:

> Naturally, the cadastral maps began to be used for identifying the land parcels referred to in the deeds recorded in the deeds registers. Thus the cadastral survey which had originated as a device of record for the administrative convenience of the State came to serve the needs of individual proprietors for parcel identification in their land dealing. Indeed, though the original and principal purpose of the cadastral record is not to prove ownership but to assess the liability for tax and determine the responsibility for payment, it clearly begins to provide evidence of land rights if it is kept up to date by entering changes of ownership in it. The courts will tend to accept it as evidence to an extent depending on the accuracy of its original compilation and the efficiency with which it has been maintained. Thus the land records of the rural areas of the Indian subcontinent, compiled initially purely for fiscal purposes, are evidence of 'presumptive title'; the title is good until positively rebutted.

Investigations carried out by the Bureau of the International Office of Cadastres and Land Records show, that in practically all the cadastral countries having also a system of land registration, the property concerned is identified by its description in the cadastre. This presupposes however that the cadastre is rather complete. Where this is not the case, as in Spain–Portugal and most of Latin America, the registration of deeds is practically independent of the cadastre and without the unique identification.

The cadastre has been used not only to enhance the deeds registration but also to facilitate the change from the deed to the title registration system. The title registration may use the cadastre identification system to establish entries for each property. The technical prerequisites for title registration are thus readily available. What is still needed to take the leap is the will to do it.

Several countries have done so. The most conspicuous change was made in Germany after its unification in 1871. A law was enacted in Prussia, stipulating that no land transaction may be valid unless a proper conveyance was registered, and a register of title was compiled from the existing material within the next few years. Other German states followed. Finally, in 1899, the 'Buergerliches Gesetzbuch' (Civil Code) ruled that an entry in the appropriate register was to be the sole admissible evidence of title to land throughout Germany. The same step of progressing to a register of title was later on taken in Europe by countries such as Switzerland, Austria and Sweden.

The development of a complete and efficient cadastre influences thus the evolution of a (legal) land registration system. There is also a trend in the opposite direction. The country which has developed an efficient (legal) land registration system might wish to enhance it with cadastral surveys and systematic compilation of register index maps from existing maps, aerial pictures combined with ground surveys, etc. This trend has been evident in countries like New Zealand and several Australian states (Williamson 1986). In the first step the register was completed with properties not yet recorded in it. Next, the different maps were brought together, the earlier unsurveyed areas were identified and demarcated by some kind of schematic surveys, and register index plans were prepared, and connections with general reference and control nets were established.

3.4 Different structures

Differences in initial conditions, development strategies and stages have given rise to substantial differences in types and combinations of cadastral and land registration systems all over the world. Many countries in the Third World, but also some highly developed ones like the USA, have weak and far from complete land information systems. Countries with complete-coverage systems differ in system structures. The main structure types are schematically illustrated in Fig. 3.3.

Countries like Sweden (case A) may have a basic real property register identifying the property and providing some description of area, land use and the origin of the property. Upon this base other registers can be built, especially for such purposes as assessment, land registration, and so on. The property register is administered by land surveying agencies; the assessment register by regional/local bodies; and the land/title register by local courts or other juridical institutions. All the registers, though different in purposes, use the common land property identifier from the real property register.

Other countries (case B) may have built their systems on (legal) land registers with or without map support. On these land registers some kinds of systematic cadastral plans *may* have been developed.

Yet other countries (case C) may have developed in the first place a systematic cadastre for taxation purposes, while (legal) land registration was initially sporadic and not linked to the cadastre. In these countries, land registers *may*

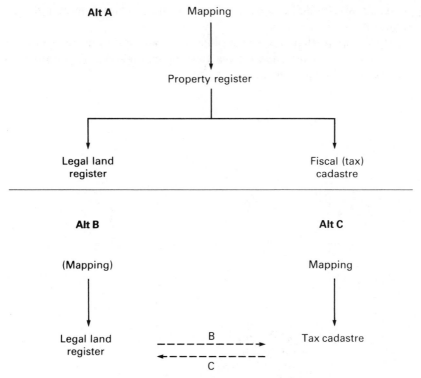

Fig. 3.3   Alternative ways of building cadastral/land registration systems

later on have adopted the cadastral land unit for property identification and finally evolved into the title registration systems with special entries for each cadastral land unit.

In countries with cases B and C the linkage between cadastral and land registration systems may be strong, weak or non-existent. Irrespective of these differences, the land registration and cadastral systems are almost always administered by different authorities.

Much can be said about the necessity, or lack of it, of these different registers and administrations. They are more a product of historical and institutional developments than of rational design. A country should not be advised, in building its own land registration and information systems, to follow the same winding development path. The relevant question should be: How can land records best be built up, arranged and maintained in order to confer maximum benefit in reaching different goals without incurring excessive costs?

This question has gained relevance even in countries with a long history of land records. Cadastral systems are no longer of interest only for taxation purposes; the land tax has been losing its relative importance in Western Europe. Land registration has developed well beyond the singular purpose of protecting private interests in land. It has increasingly been recognized that the two systems should be treated as components of a larger, more integrated land information system.

Before we go further into the problems of system design, we will take a look at the results achieved in Europe and some Anglo-Saxon countries. We will also discuss benefit questions.

4

Cadastral and land registration systems in Europe

As the next chapter is devoted to land registration in Anglo-Saxon and English speaking countries, it is natural to include England there. This chapter will concentrate on the rest of Europe.

The subject of cadastral and land registration systems in Europe has been dealt with in a paper by J. Henssen (1987). Much of Sections 4.1–4.4 are based on this paper. We have already touched on some significant elements of European developments but will now go into more detail.

Henssen places special emphasis on the distinction between Western and Eastern Europe. But there are major variations even within Western Europe. England has already been mentioned as a special case. The Northern and Southern parts of Europe also differ in many respects. We shall, therefore, start by treating the subject under four headings: Western, Northern, Southern and Eastern Europe. After that we shall try to point out some lessons to be drawn from the past as well as some common, current and probable future trends.

4.1 Western Europe

For historical reasons, there are basic similarities among all the cadastres of Western Europe. They are all, in one way or another, based on the principles of the French cadastre as defined by Napoleon early in the nineteenth century. A basic principle was that it should consist of two main parts: a verbal description and a map showing the locations and boundaries of all land units. The maps were established systematically, area by area, by relatively uniform cadastral surveys, which produced not only the maps but also the field notes on which they were based. The unique cadastral number of each land unit – normally the parcel rather than the farm unit – served as a link between map and description. Since the main purpose was taxation, the original cadastre was arranged according to the names of the owners, showing each owner's parcels with area, land use, quality and value. Later, another cadastre emerged parallel to this one, arranged according to the numbers of the parcels.

An important feature of these developments is the connection between the cadastre and the land register. In Germany, Austria, Switzerland and the Netherlands, there is nowadays a very close link between cadastres and land registers. In The Netherlands, both are maintained by the same organization in common offices. In the other countries mentioned above, the legal units used in the land registers are also identical with the cadastral units or combinations of them. Because of the unique definitions in the cadastral records and maps, it has been possible to introduce systems of title registration with a high degree of security and reliability in all these countries.

In France – the mother country of the cadastre – the unification of the cadastre and the land register has not progressed as far. For one thing, the French cadastre is not as comprehensive nor is it maintained in quite the same way as in the aforementioned countries. It also has less legal validity, and is still mainly a fiscal cadastre lacking the very close link between cadastre and legal land registers.

Naturally, the French system has also exerted great influence in the former colonies such as most of the countries of North and West Africa. In these countries, cadastres and land registers ('Livre Foncier') generally cover only a minor portion of the land, mostly in urban areas. Generally, registration is essentially voluntary (but compulsory in certain cases such as grants from state owned land). The land register is normally a title register with a folio for each parcel. If someone wants to register his land, he has to apply to the registrar. His application will then be officially announced during a prescribed period, and the land must then be surveyed and demarcated in the presence of neighbours and other involved parties. After the deadline for appeal has passed, the land unit is inscribed in the register, and the owner is given a certificate of title.

A common trait in all of Western Europe is that the cadastre provides systematic coverage of the entire territory, and that collected and recorded data are continually updated. Parcels are described according to their uses, square measures and taxation values, their buildings and topography; ownerships are recorded; links to other administrative registers and files are established. A general trend is that the original fiscal aspect of the cadastre is becoming less and less pronounced, while its role as the basis of a general land information system is assuming increasing importance.

In all Western European countries, cadastral maps are used for many purposes besides the original one. In Switzerland, for example, the towns often produce extremely accurate municipal maps based on cadastral information. The integration of cadastral surveys with other kinds of large-scale mapping for urban purposes is a common trend in other countries within the region as well.

With regard to the cadastral survey, there has generally been a trend

0 1 2 3 4 5 6 7 8 9 10 11 12 13 14 15 16 17 18 19 20 21 22 23 24 25 26 27 28 29 30 31 32 33 34 35 36 37 38 39 40 41 42 43 44 45 46 47 48 49

Gemeinde Heurled

Eigentümer: K l e i n , Georg, geb. Bahnhofstr. 4

Vb 54/4972 K l e i n , Johann, Landwirt, Hf. Zwölfergut Richter, geb. Bahnhofstr. 4 i.i.?

VL 21/1973: F u c h s Heinrich, Elektriker, Eichenweg 3

GB 3/45

Betand Nummer 137

Seite 1 bis ..

Auswärtige Gemeindebuchteile	Nummer des Flurstücks	Lage Gebäudebesitz	Nutzungart	Fläche ha a qm	Ertragmeßzahl	Gesamtfläche des Flurstücks ha a qm	Fortführung VN oder VL Nr./Jahrgang	Bemerkungen Gebäudebesitz fremder Eigentümer
1	- 2	3	4	5	6	7	8	9
	116/2	Eichenweg 3				24 00		
		Wohnhaus, Werkstätte,	Hf	9 00				
		Hofraum						
			G	15 00	750			
	116/3	Eichenweg 5				24 50		
			Hf	10 50				Wohnhaus, Schmiede,
								Hofraum, Lagerplatz
				14 00	700			des Uche Arton, Schmied,
								Eichenweg 5
								Erbbaurecht GB 4/65

Fig. 4.1 Extract from a German cadastre (*Liegenschaftsbuch*)

31

towards using increasingly accurate methods, and at the same time, assigning more and more weight to the demarcation of boundaries and to agreements between the owners; that is, there is growing stress on the fixing of boundaries. A tendency which, to some extent, runs counter to these developments is the widespread use of photogrammetric methods for cadastral purposes, especially in connection with initial cadastral surveys of an area. Due to the deficient quality of some original surveys and to poor maintenance later on, continuous re-surveying has often been necessary.

While cadastral maps were originally of the 'island map' type, depicting only the cadastral block or section in question, they now increasingly take the form of 'comprehensive maps' covering a standard-sized map sheet. This is partly a consequence of the transformation from taxation cadastres to multipurpose cadastres. It is also due to the fact that nowadays all cadastral surveys in Western Europe are adapted to a national grid with a common co-ordinate system. It is, therefore, also possible to integrate cadastral surveying and general topographical surveying, and to use a common sheet division for both types of surveys.

An interesting developmental trend in some Western countries is the establishment of a building register linked to the cadastre. In most countries, principal buildings are represented on the cadastral maps. The registers can be expanded to include substantial information about the buildings. In the Federal Republic of Germany, for example, an attempt is being made to establish a register of buildings as an additional, integrated part of the cadastre. This is quite in line with the general trend of making the cadastre the basis of an expanded land information system.

The administration of the cadastre is organized in a variety of ways in different countries. In Germany and The Netherlands, the cadastral authorities were initially government officers connected to the Ministry of Finance. But as a consequence of the expanded function of the cadastre as the basis of a multipurpose land information system, the Dutch cadastre, for example, was reorganized as a separate division within the Ministry of Housing, Physical Planning and the Environment. In other countries like France, Switzerland and Belgium, the principal work of cadastral surveying is left to licensed surveyors.

4.2 Northern Europe

Of the Scandinavian countries, Denmark has the system most similar to the Western European ones (Stubkjaer 1981). Denmark has long had a comprehensive cadastral map, covering the whole country and connected to a common reference system. Cadastral surveys for subdivisions, etc., are made by private surveyors. However, the records are kept, and the cadastral maps are maintained by a central government office in Copenhagen called 'Matrikel-kontoret'. The cadastre is closely integrated with the land registration system, which is of the title registration type.

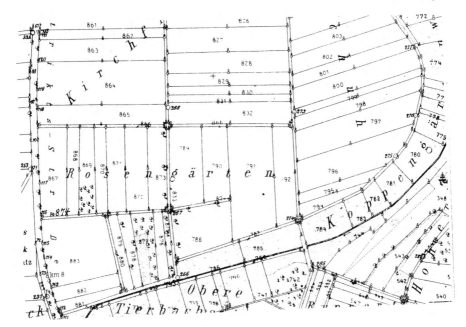

Fig. 4.2   Extract from a German cadastral map

The same close integration is also found in Sweden and Finland, which both have systems of title registration based on cadastral units. In these countries the cadastre has developed gradually from simple taxation records loosely linked to maps, to a comprehensive system with a high degree of reliability. In Sweden, the urban cadastres were linked with large-scale maps at an early date. Later, a photo map in the scale of 1:10000, showing all land units in rural areas with their boundaries, was established as a registration index map (see Fig. 4.3). In Sweden the urban and rural systems have now been combined into a common register, while different types of records for rural and urban regions still exist in Finland. Apart from this, the Finnish and Swedish cadastres are similarly structured.

In Sweden the cadastre has been further integrated with the land register through automation. One single agency, the Central Board for Real Estate Data (CFD), collects and transforms selected cadastral and land register information for automatic data processing. The regional cadastral and land registration offices are still responsible for data collection. They have on-line links with CFD, and are empowered to change the records in case of subdivision, transfer of ownership, etc. CFD is responsible for issuing all certificates as well as for all communications with other authorities using real-estate data. Duplication of effort is thereby avoided. The time needed to produce the legal documents and distribute them to those concerned has also been shor-

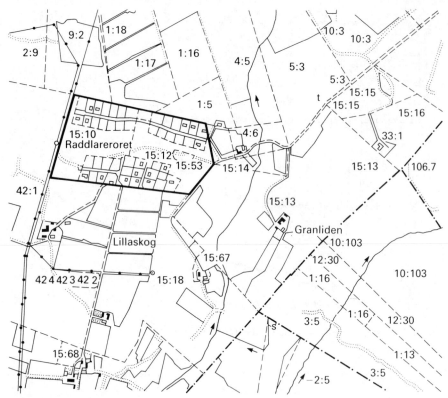

Fig. 4.3   Extract from Swedish cadastral map

tened substantially. The system is now (1991) operational in the greatest part of the country, and will be complete in about five years.

Norway has not previously had a proper cadastral system, relying instead on old tax records, only partially supported by maps. The country has, however, decided to establish an automated system – the GAB system – providing data on land units, addresses and buildings. Its main purpose is to provide information, not to serve as a legal basis for taxation, land registration, etc. In the long run, however, it will probably assume an importance far beyond its role in the dissemination of information.

4.3   Southern Europe

Spain and Italy were also influenced by the Napoleonic cadastre, and adopted basically similar systems. However, they were only partially developed, and the Spanish system especially does not provide comprehensive, national coverage. The link between cadastre and land registration is weak. The two records are administered by different authorities, and the descriptions of the land in the land register do not always refer to the cadastral units. The link between cadastre and register is, therefore, not primarily the parcel designation, but rather the name of the owner. This is, of course, an obstacle to further integration.

The fiscal nature of the cadastres is more predominant in Southern than in Western Europe. As buildings are important objects for taxation, Italy has established a modern building register as part of the cadastre.

Greece does not have a comprehensive, homogeneous, national cadastre, but the problem has been studied, and a governmental decision to establish a nationwide system appears forthcoming.

4.4 Eastern Europe

In some parts of Eastern Europe, especially Czechoslovakia and Poland, conventional, pre-war cadastres still exist. They have, however, now been developed along other lines. Here, as in other parts of Eastern Europe, efforts have been concentrated mainly on establishing an economically and ecologically oriented land information system. Information needs no longer concern parcels, taxes and owners, but rather environmental and agricultural resources. The classification units are based on natural and technical factors such as land use, soil and ecology, climate and water supply. In Eastern Europe too, there are strong tendencies to develop the cadastral registers into multipurpose systems, and to establish information bases not only for production planning, but also for regional planning and environmental protection. Generally it might be observed that the reorganization of the property structure in Eastern Europe has brought about such major changes that completely new land records have had to be compiled. In countries which already had well-developed, 'conventional' cadastres, these have served as the basis for further modernization.

4.5 General trends

Today's European cadastral/land registration systems are all strongly influenced by the land information concept. In short, the main trends can be expressed in the following terms: multiple uses, automation, geocodes and digitization.

We have already touched on the concept of *multiple uses*. The cadastre and the land register were each originally designed for *one* purpose: taxation and security in rights. But almost from the very start, the information provided and the maps produced were found to be very useful for other purposes as well. Only during recent decades, however, has this point been stressed in the technical design of cadastres and land registers. Modern society has developed into an information society, which both requires, and has the ability to produce, accurate information. However, if the information – not least spatial information – is to be convenient to handle, it must be linked to identifiable spatial units. The cadastral land unit is one such unit which is a suitable basis for much information – not only concerning the land itself, but also the people living on the land and many of their activities.

This does *not*, however, mean that cadastre/land register themselves should contain the necessary land information. On the contrary, all experience shows that both cadastres and land registers should be kept simple, and concentrate only on the data required for their particular purposes. The essential thing is the uniquely defined land unit, which can be used as a key for integrating many different records, thus making available a vast amount of relevant land information.

It is, however, difficult to achieve such a high level of integration when all records are kept manually. Two records such as a cadastre and a land register could certainly be made to influence each other considerably, and to function as one source of information. But in order to advance from here to an efficient, fully integrated system consisting of several different sub-systems, *automation* is essential.

Practically all European countries are today working on the problem of automating relevant land records – first and foremost cadastres and land registers. The main reason is not to achieve integration, but rather to make each separate record function efficiently. Increased integration is, however, a very important by-product. No country has yet achieved the complete automation of its cadastral/land registration systems. But this is merely a question of time. Sweden is probably the country which has come furthest in constructing an automated, on-line, integrated system of cadastral, land registry, land taxation and population records. Most European countries are definitely on their way in the same direction.

Another clear trend is the conversion of land-related information into spatial systems. The information must be precisely located in order to be of greatest use. One method is by *geocoding*. If the land unit is assigned coordinates in the national grid, all land-related information can be spatially defined. The system used by Sweden, for example, introduces the co-ordinate of the central point of the land unit as well as the co-ordinate of the principal building – graphically determined – into the cadastral records. If in future all boundary points were determined graphically or numerically by coordinates, and the coordinates were inserted into the cadastral database, this would, of course, make possible a similar spatial determination of information.

This is what is now happening in most European countries. Starting with the most highly urbanized areas, the cadastral maps are increasingly being *digitized*. This is motivated mainly by the great opportunities it creates for using the same database for producing maps in different scales and with different combinations of separate 'layers' – greater freedom to present spatial information in a flexible way. At the same time the manual production methods can be automated. This is a natural step in the age of automatic data processing.

Digitization also renders a solution to the need, common to all European countries, of *integrating cadastral data with data on utilities*. Utilities such as water, sewerage, electricity and telecommunications are becoming increasingly complex; demands for efficient maintenance and management are increasing; and there is always a danger that utilities will be damaged during different kinds of excavation. For these reasons, there is an obvious need for a total approach to the surveying and recording of utilities. Utilities will be a natural element in the system of digitized, automated land information (see Fig. 4.4).

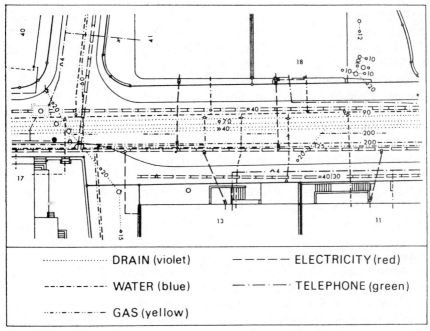

────────────── DRAIN (violet)   ─ ─ ─ ─ ─ ELECTRICITY (red)

─── ─── ─── WATER (blue)   ─ ·─ ·─ · TELEPHONE (green)

──·─··─··─·─ GAS (yellow)

Fig. 4.4 Utility map, showing underground services (from Dale 1976)

4.6 Some European experiences

With the exception of the very essential contributions made by Torrens and the Australian states, the main development of cadastral and land-registration systems has taken place in Europe. Even though times and conditions have changed, some lessons might be drawn from these European experiences: lessons which might be useful for countries about to develop modern systems of cadastres and land registration.

In his overview of basic elements in a cadastral system, F. Kurandt (1955) starts by saying: 'Benzenberg's exhortation should be repeated in the introduction to every treatment of the cadastre: The main point of a cadastre is that it will be ready.'

The cadastre will be largely worthless unless it is substantially complete within a particular geographical area. One of the greatest achievements of the Napoleonic cadastre was that from the very start, and regardless of the nature of the land, it provided a complete record of all land units within the area – including unique identification – and defined these units on comprehensive maps. To attain this goal, cadastres and land registers must be kept simple, and must *concentrate on the essentials*. Furthermore, the work must have a *solid foundation*. Even if conditions change over time, if new aspects become relevant, if new political winds start to blow, the process must still continue along the same main lines until it is finished. This presupposes long-term political support, that is, *costs must be kept reasonable in relation to expected medium-term benefits*. This is more important than producing a product which is technically perfect. There are many examples in Europe of cadastral systems which have been stopped or delayed because of faltering political support. Even in France – the cradle of the European cadastre – it was difficult to complete and maintain the cadastre.

Another lesson is that in the long run, there will be *no single-purpose land records*. Cadastres were created with the aim of improving the basis for land taxation, and land registers were established to make land transactions more secure. Initially they were independent of each other, but they have become increasingly interrelated, and are used with increasing frequency for purposes other than the original ones. It has taken a long time, however, for most European countries to reach this point. Difficulties arose since the original records were not designed as parts of common information systems, and because their maintenance was entrusted to different organizations. It is, therefore, essential that the goals of *multiple usage* and *integration* be adopted at the conception of a modern cadastral/land information system.

If land records develop along these lines, the chosen cadastral unit will become important in many connections. If legal land registration as well as other land records are based on the same unit, the unit will assume considerable legal and practical importance. In most countries with well-developed cadastral/land information systems, subdivision or other changes in the cadastral unit require formal legal proceedings and, as a rule, re-surveying. The proceedings often include an assessment of whether the change conforms to land control principles or urban planning rules. Private changes or subdivisions made without formal proceedings are not accepted or given legal status. A conclusion drawn from European experiences is that *the land unit tends to become a legal entity protected by law*.

The increasing importance of this unit can also be demonstrated from another point of view. In the past, cadastral and other records were usually arranged according to the names of the current owners. The records in many countries are still indexed in this way, which makes searches difficult as ownership changes. In Western countries the cadastres/land registers are increasingly being indexed according to the more enduring entity of the land unit itself, identified by maps and unit number. This unit also serves as a key for integrating other records into the system. *Land records should be based on defined land units, not on persons.*

As mentioned above, a cadastre/land register must cover an entire geographical area in order to provide essential benefits from a public point of view. Seen from the viewpoint of the private owner, even a sporadic register can be useful, as it can provide protection for *his* interests. The costs should then be borne by the private individuals concerned rather than by the public. There are no impelling reasons for public subsidies for sporadic land registers or other land records.

To fulfil the public goal of establishing complete land records within the area in question, *the inclusion of every land unit must be compulsory.* European experiences demonstrate overwhelmingly that voluntary registration is insufficient for establishing comprehensive land records, even in the long term. To satisfy the public goal, the establishment of the records must generally be undertaken *systematically, area by area.* In practice this means *that the costs of establishing the records should be borne mainly by the government.* This is quite logical as comprehensive records are primarily a public interest, at least in the short term. This also applies to mapping. The preparation of comprehensive, registration index maps cannot be financed by private landowners.

In developing countries, the resources available for establishing different kinds of land information systems are usually meagre. This was also true in many European countries during the nineteenth century. Therefore we have many examples of how cadastres/land registers were started in a very simple way, and then were developed progressively into smoothly operating systems through gradual upgrading and improvement. Sweden and Finland provide two such examples. The German adaptation of a system of titles instead of a system of deeds at the end of the nineteenth century is another example. What Doeble (1985) calls a *progressive* cadastre, starting on a sound but simple, inexpensive basis, and developing further when resources and technology permit, is a possible course of action. In line with this progressive approach is the desire to make the chosen system *flexible.* Every land information system must be able to adapt to new developments and new aims in the future. It must, therefore, be possible to add new types of data, and to make changes. This applies to the technical details as well. For example the numbering system of the land units must be constructed so as not to become too cumbersome to use even after long chains of subdivisions. This is unfortunately not always taken into consideration at the start, and may be difficult to change later on.

An important lesson from the European experience is that *very careful consideration must be given to maintenance and updating from the very start.* Too many European cadastres/land registers have had weak periods during which their usefulness was seriously impaired at least temporarily because of insufficient updating. One of the most important factors in this respect is that the registration of all transactions in land be compulsory. For transactions involving a change in boundaries, there must be simple but mandatory procedures to ensure that all changes are surveyed and mapped before registration takes place.

Finally, the rapid rate of change in existing European systems, especially during the last two decades, shows clearly that the design of cadastral/land registration systems must be *future oriented*. This applies to technical aspects as well as to the fundamental principles of the system. Less-developed countries must, therefore, carefully consider and evaluate all experiences which can be obtained from other countries. An example is automation. It is often doubtful whether it should be introduced from the beginning. On the other hand, it is bound to come sooner or later. This means that today's systems and structures must be planned in such a way that necessary changes are easy to make tomorrow.

5

Land registration in English speaking countries

Systems of land registration in Anglo-Saxon countries are of interest for several reasons. First, these systems have had a strong influence in the former colonies and dominions. Furthermore, they differ in many ways from the continental system, in large part because until recently the cadastre has been almost unknown in the English-speaking world.

There are well-documented studies about both the development and the present state of English land law and land registration. The development of English land law is treated, for example, by A. W. B. Simpson (1961). Dowson and Sheppard (1968) and S. Rowton Simpson (1976) give very valuable documentation about land law and land registration in countries influenced by the English system. Ruoff (1968) and Love (1968) discuss the English and Australian registration systems. Williamson (1986) examines recent trends in the Australian system. The following presentation is heavily indebted to the above sources.

5.1 Land registration in England

As we noted earlier, one of the oldest land records was compiled in England – the famous Domesday Survey, completed in 1086. The Domesday Book, a record of information collected for the levying of taxes, was remarkable for its time, a kind of cadastre without map. However, the Domesday Survey was unique and was never reviewed or maintained. There has never been a cadastre, in the European sense, in England or in those countries that adopted English traditions. This chapter will, therefore, discuss mainly the development and the present state of the legal *land registration system*.

The basis of any system of land registration is, of course, the legal codes pertaining to land. Clearly, before land rights can be registered, they must be defined. But the details of English land law are too complicated and difficult for us to examine here. A few basic facts, however, are needed for discussion. In English legal theory only the sovereign can own land. In the eyes of the law a private person can thus be nothing more than a tenant on the land. Tenancy rights, as recognized in the law of 1925, had been reduced to two: (a) fee simple absolute (or freehold) and (b) a term of years absolute (leasehold). A lease may be defined as a contract granting the exclusive right to possession of land for a fixed or determinable period. There is no legal limit to the term of years. Leases for 999 years are common, but the majority of leases are likely to be considerably shorter. A special type of lease is the building lease: the lessee leases vacant land for which he pays a ground rent, agreeing in addition to erect a building on the site according to certain specifications. A typical building lease is for 99 years. These features of English land law have influenced the attitudes towards, and practices regarding, land ownership and leaseholds in many of the former dominions and colonies.

Land registration as such had great difficulty winning acceptance in England. Rights in land were commonly transferred by private conveyance. The chain of deeds, which gave a person 'a good root of title to land' had to be submitted before conveyance could be completed, therefore, few Englishmen contemplated buying or selling land without the aid of a solicitor.

Many attempts were made to establish registration to make land conveyance both simpler and more secure. But such attempts never really succeeded. In the middle of the nineteenth century, however, a commission's recommendation that titles be registered led to the Land Registry Act of 1862. This was later followed by the Land Transfer Act of 1875.

In one respect these Acts were very modern, differing little in fact from the present law. An important difference existed, however, between the 1862 and 1875 laws regarding the concept of boundaries. According to the Act of 1862, a precise definition of boundaries was necessary before registration, while the 1875 Act introduced the concept of general boundaries, still the prevailing one in England. The term 'general boundary' means that the exact line of the boundary is left undetermined 'as for instance whether it includes a hedge or wall and ditch, or runs along the centre of a wall or fence, or its inner or outer face, or how far it runs within or beyond it; or whether or not the land registered includes the whole or any portion of an adjoining road or stream' (Land Registration Rules 1925 r. 278).

However, both the 1862 and the 1875 Acts failed completely to achieve their purpose. In 40 years fewer than 1000 titles were registered. The main reason for this lack of interest was certainly that registration was voluntary, with costs being borne by the owner, who might be unaware of the advantages of registration even if he was aware that registration was possible. The government showed no interest in encouraging registration, and the English solicitors were hardly enthusiastic advocates for registration, scarcely surprising since they derived a major portion of their income from conveyance fees in the transfer of land rights.

A new Land Transfer Act of 1897 introduced the possibility of selective compulsory registration. Under this Act the registration of title could be made compulsory on sales in designated areas at the request of a county council. By 1902 this measure had been applied to the County of London, but registration remained purely voluntary in the rest of England and Wales. The question of the reforming of the codes governing registration was complex because of its link with the obvious need for reform of the land law in general.

In 1925, however, a package of new land laws was enacted. One of these was the Land Registration Act, which made registration of titles compulsory within designated areas. These areas were gradually extended so that today all of England is covered. Registration is, however, still sporadic since properties are registered only when the land is sold or subject to a long lease. It will, therefore, be a long time before the bulk of the land is registered. Generally, three main objections can be raised against a sporadic system of registration of titles:

- It takes a long time to complete the register.

- Registration costs per unit are high. It is obviously much cheaper to survey and delimit the properties within an area all at once than to do it piecemeal.

- Only systematic registration can provide an overview of all the existing parcels and titles within an area. Such an overview is essential for such purposes as planning, land administration, land taxation, etc.

To a certain degree these objections can also be raised against the English system. However, the last two objections are less important in England than elsewhere because of the *Ordnance map* and the *general boundaries* system.

The Ordnance Survey established (essentially between 1853 and 1893) a topographic map of the whole of England, normally on a scale of 1:2500 for rural areas and 1:1250 for urban areas. The map shows hedges, ditches, roads, etc., that is, in most cases all the natural boundaries around a certain property. The maps are continually revised. Except for newly developed properties, it is often possible to identify a sold property directly on the map. Accordingly, the Land Registration Rules of 1925 state that 'the Ordnance map shall be the basis of all registered descriptions of land'. Because of the general boundary rule, the Ordnance map satisfies the need for the identification of properties in most cases. Descriptions contained in private deeds are, however, not infrequently inaccurate or ambiguous. In such cases as well as in areas of new development, the Ordnance Survey Department collaborates with the Land Registry and makes *ad hoc* surveys.

There has been considerable discussion about the general boundary rule, especially as to whether it should be extended to areas formerly under British influence. It has generally not been extended beyond Britain because conditions elsewhere differ from those in Britain. A defender of the general boundary system in England can point to the fact that although anyone may, at any time, have his boundaries surveyed and described with meticulous care at his own expense, only one person in a million actually wishes to go through this process (Ruoff 1968).

After an area has been designated for title registration, any person who buys unregistered freehold land or acquires an unregistered lease for a term of 40 or more years must apply to the Land Registry for registration of his title within two months of the completion of the transaction. The same compulsory registration rule applies to subsequent transactions. In the case of the first registration, the former owner has to submit satisfactory evidence to the registrar that he has sound title and is thus the real owner. Once a property is registered, the government guarantees the title as listed in the register. In cases of loss due to fraud or to a mistake in the register, compensation can be received from an insurance fund. However, few claims have been made to date, and the total cost of the insurance fund since the guarantee was introduced is less than £100 000 (Ruoff 1968). (Figures 5.1 and 5.2 illustrate, respectively, an extract from an English land register and a land certificate.)

5.2 Land registration in Australia

English law and English practices exerted, of course, a great influence upon those countries settled or dominated by Britain. However, the legislation introduced by Sir Robert Torrens in South Australia in 1858 (the other Australian states soon followed) was even more important. This registration system – usually called the Torrens system – is fundamentally a title register. It applied to all land alienated by the Crown after the introduction of the Transfer of Land Act developed by Torrens. The main principles are presented below.

Two grants are issued for each piece of land at the first registration, one is called the original, the other the duplicate. The original Crown grant is held by the Office of Titles in the Register book, which is open to the public, and the duplicate is issued to the grantee. The grant describes the land by means of a diagram, which appears on both the original and the duplicate. It also gives the name of the grantee and his occupation; the price paid for the property; any limitations, special reservations, or conditions; and finally the area and its Crown description. For purposes of record, each title is filed under a given volume and folio number (Love 1968).

If the original grantee subsequently transfers the land, the name of the new registered owner is merely endorsed on the back of both the original and the duplicate Crown grants with a reference to the registered number of the deed of transfer. The Office of Titles then enters the name of the new registered owner in an index with the relevant volume and folio numbers. If the transfer covers only a part of the property, a sketch plan is prepared by the Office of Titles indicating the boundaries and dimensions of the section being transferred and giving the registered transfer number. This sketch is attached to the grant, and endorsements are made on the back of the grant.

A main feature of the Torrens system is thus that the land in question is

H.M. LAND REGISTRY

TITLE NUMBER   00002
This register consists of   2   *pages*

A. PROPERTY REGISTER

containing the description of the registered land and the estate comprised in the Title

ADMINISTRATIVE AREA	PARISH OR PLACE
(County, County Borough, etc.)	
BLANKSHIRE	BROXMORE

The Freehold land shown and edged with red on the plan of the above Title filed at the Registry

registered on 12 October 1934 known as 2 Moon Street.

B. PROPRIETORSHIP REGISTER

stating nature of the Title, name, address and description of the proprietor of the land and any entries affecting the right of disposal thereof

TITLE ABSOLUTE

Entry number	Proprietor, etc.	Application number and remarks
1.	JOHN SMITH, Printer and WILLIAM BROWN, Engineer, both of 4 Moon Street, Broxmore, Blankshire, registered on 1 February 1968.	Price paid £900.
2.	RESTRICTION registered on 1 February 1968:-No disposition by one proprietor of the land (being the survivor of joint proprietors and not being a trust corporation) under which capital money arises is to be registered except under an order of the registrar or of the Court.	
3.	CAUTION in favour of Jesse Turnbull of 30 Park Way, Torquay, Devon, Electrical Engineer, registered on 20 February 1968.	4563/68

Page 2

C. CHARGES REGISTER

containing charges, incumbrances, etc., adversely affecting the land and registered dealings therewith

TITLE NUMBER   00002

Entry number	The date at the beginning of each entry is the date on which the entry was made on this edition of the register.	Application number and remarks
1.	1 February 1968-A Conveyance of the land in this title dated 30 September 1934 and made between (1) Mary Brown (Vendor) and (2) Harold Robins (Purchaser) contains the following covenants:- "The Purchaser hereby covenants with the Vendor for the benefit of her adjoining land known as 27, 29, 31, 33 and 35 Cabot Road to observe and perform the stipulations and conditions contained in the Schedule hereto. THE SCHEDULE before referred to 1. No building to be erected on the land shall be used other than as a private dwellinghouse. 2. No building to be erected as aforesaid shall be converted into or used as flats, maisonettes or separate tenements or as a boarding house. 3. The garden ground of the premises shall at all times be kept in neat and proper order and condition and shall not be converted to any other use whatsoever. 4. Nothing shall be done or permitted on the premises which may be a nuisance or annoyance to the adjoining houses or to the neighbourhood."	
2.	1 February 1968-LEASE dated 25 July 1935 to Charles Jones for 99 years from 24 June 1935 at the rent of £45.	Lessee's title registered under 00003
3.	1 February 1968-NOTICE of Deposit of Land Certificate with Mid Town Bank Limited of 2 High Street, Broxmore, Blankshire, registered on 1 February 1968.	3212/68

Fig. 5.1   Extract of English register in land certificate

H. M. LAND REGISTRY

NATIONAL GRID PLAN   SF 6205   SECTION   C
(BLANKSHIRE)

Scale   1/1250

BROXMORE PARISH

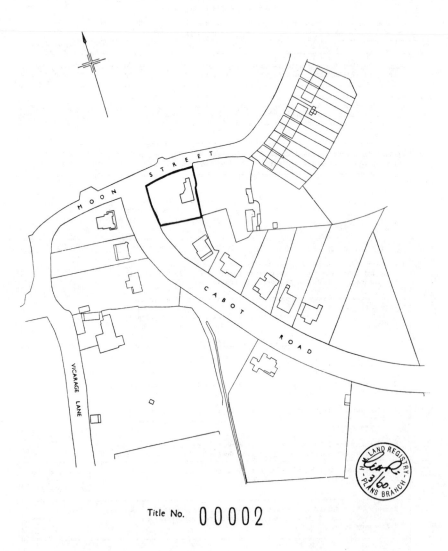

Title No. 0 0 0 0 2

(The thick line hereon represents the red edging on the Certificate Plan.)

Fig. 5.2 Plan in English land certificate

identified on a map appended to the certificate of title and that the certificate of title gives details of ownership as well as a description of the land, with appropriate reference to easements, encumbrances, and other conditions (see Fig. 5.3). All transfers must be applied for, examined, and registered at the Office of Titles. This mandatory requirement is an important feature of the Torrens system, for the Crown can thus guarantee the new ownership. Guarantees are supported by an insurance fund, which, however, has rarely been used.

The English system and the Torrens system have many similarities. However, some differences exist between them (see Simpson 1976, p. 78):

- The Torrens register is made up of Crown grants or subdivisions of Crown grants; the English system registers sales after a thorough investigation and before the first property registration.

- The Torrens register does not include Crown land, while in England there is no difference between Crown land and private land as far as registration is concerned.

- In England the 'general boundaries' principle is applied; in the Torrens system all registered land is surveyed and a plan showing the essential indicators of the boundaries is drawn on the certificate of title.

- The English system is concerned only with the current ownership and property boundaries so that the register is in effect an index-card system, while in the Torrens system all entries from the time of the first registration are preserved in folio volumes.

The Torrens system does not cover land granted before the system was legally established. For such old land grants, registration is voluntary. Therefore, two systems still exist side by side in Australian states. The majority of transfers follow the Torrens system, but others take place without registration in the form of private conveyances, where lawyers from both sides draw up the documents needed and effect the transfer. There have been efforts, however, to bring all land under title registration. In 1924 New Zealand enacted a law which, within 20 years, brought all the outstanding titles into the register. Similar legislation was later adopted by several Australian states. By requiring systematic registration, which includes the necessary title searches and mapping, Australia is well on the way to achieving a complete system of land registration.

The completion of this system will, of course, also make it easier to use registration as a means of establishing a land information system based on registered land units. The Torrens system in itself does not produce cadastral maps for large areas, only maps of individual properties. During the 1970s, however, the focus in Australia changed to cadastral mapping, with all surveys being integrated in a general control grid, and with survey plans designed to cover not only the individual land units but also whole areas. The

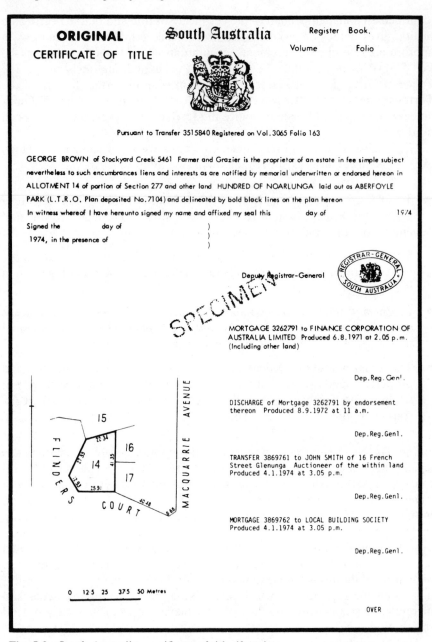

Fig. 5.3 South Australia, certificate of title (front)

1980s saw the beginning of the creation of digital cadastral databases (Williamson 1986).

5.3   Land registration in other English speaking countries

The Torrens system has also had great impact outside New Zealand and Australia, both as a concept and in practice, especially in Anglo-Saxon countries and in areas formerly dominated by Britain. The former British colonies in East Africa have introduced title registration systems influenced by the Torrens concept. Normally they are applied only to minor parts of the countries. In Kenya, however, title registration is gradually being extended throughout the entire country (Lawrance Mission 1966).

Kenya is very interesting as an example of a developing country where systematic title registration is being implemented on a large scale. Between the two world wars, population pressures led to more intensive cultivation and increasing private ownership of land. Customary tribal supremacy over the land was weakened, and land also became increasingly subdivided and fragmented. Influenced partly by the Mau Mau revolt against British rule, the government decided to improve land holdings through consolidation and at the same time give the tenant secure rights to his land through title registration.

This process was compulsory within designated areas, starting with the Central Province. After an area, usually a district, was declared an adjudication area, an officer was appointed, who divided the area into adjudication sections. Thereafter he established a period during which all persons claiming land rights could submit their claims, although later claims were accepted. A committee of residents was appointed for each adjudication section, with its main task being to advise the adjudication officer. For the adjudication work the Survey Department, generally using enlarged aerial photographs, prepared a topographical map with a scale of 1:2500.

In the areas of consolidation, each plot was surveyed not by a surveying authority, but by special teams of measurers trained in chain measuring. The approximate area of each plot was calculated and recorded for every owner. The committee, together with the adjudication officer, settled disputes and also decided what land was required for local public purposes. After making allocations for public areas, the committee then allocated new land to every landowner – usually one single lot with regular boundaries – equivalent in area to all his previous fragmented lots. The new boundaries were then laid out in the field and demarcated mostly by hedges, etc.

After most of the fragmented areas in the central parts of Kenya had been consolidated, the surveying groups turned their attention to the adjudication of land which should not be consolidated. Enlarged aerial photographs continued to be used as base maps. Property boundaries, if any, are identified in the field on enlarged photographs, non-visible boundaries being indicated by reference to identifiable details. Demarcation by beacons is not commonly practised, but the planting of hedges, etc., may be required. The registration map is then prepared by the Survey of Kenya by tracing the boundaries on inked photographs. Originally, this method was recommended only for flat areas, but it has also been used in hilly areas because of the high cost of other methods. According to the Registered Land Act, a registry map needs to indicate only the approximate boundaries and approximate location of individual parcels of land.

After the field work, the recording officer prepares an adjudication record. The law provides for the adjudication not only of individual rights but of group ownership, so adjudication does not necessarily promote individual ownership. In principle the adjudication record will contain not only the ownership but also the other rights of persons or groups, which while not the equivalent of ownership, are nevertheless recognized as rights either in customary law or by the statute laws of the country (leases, charges, widows' rights, etc.). When all disputed issues have been dealt with by the committee and the record is complete, it is available for inspection for 60 days at some suitable place within the area. Within that time any person can raise objections with the adjudication officer. His decisions can be appealed to the Minister within 60 days. The map and record are then sent to the land registrar.

The Land Register contains a loose-leaf record for each parcel and a loose-leaf record for each lease of a specified period exceeding two years. Each register is to be divided into three sections:

- The property section, containing a brief description of the land, together with particulars of its appurtenances and a reference to the registry map.

- The proprietorship section, containing the name and address of the proprietor and a note of any inhibition, caution or restriction affecting his right to disposition.

- The encumbrances section, containing a note of every encumbrance and every right adversely affecting the land.

The effect of registration is to secure for the proprietor absolute and indefeasible title to land subject only to the leases and other encumbrances shown in the register and to overriding interests.

Once a register has been established, it is of great importance that it be maintained to show current conditions. In Kenya, therefore, transfers, leases of at least two years, charges, and easements must be made by instruments on simple, standard forms, which are presented to the registrar. Failure to register renders the instrument ineffective against a later but registered instrument. No part of a land unit comprised in a register may be transferred unless the proprietor has first subdivided the land; for this purpose the district surveyor demarcates the new boundaries, makes a map of the subdivision, and then inserts the new boundaries on the registry map kept by the registrar. Registration is also subject to land controls. According to the Land Control

Act any transaction within a Land Control Area affecting agricultural land (sale, transfer, lease, mortgage, subdivision, etc.) shall be void unless the land control board has given its consent.

The system in Kenya is, in general, very interesting as it includes a series of measures regarding consolidation, adjudication, registration and land control, all applied on a large scale and supported by local committees. In only a short time the application of these measures has thoroughly changed the land tenure system of the country. The Kenya Registered Land Act and Rules are reprinted in Simpson 1976.

Systematic title registration also has been introduced in other former British colonies, for example Malaysia and Brunei. Their laws and systems have many similarities to those of Kenya, but it has been possible in these countries to build on older registration systems to a larger extent than was possible in Kenya. In some areas existing maps have been used in the new title registration system. Studies aimed at the automation of records are under way.

In India, many states have established cadastres for taxation purpose, something which is otherwise unusual in English speaking countries. Cadastral surveys are made systematically area by area, using the village as the unit of survey. A common procedure is described below.

The village is divided into survey fields of 5 to 10 acres. Trijunctions of survey fields are marked with stones and used for theodolite traverses. The owners are notified and ordered to show their claims on the land. Fields are then measured by chaining and by orthogonal offsetting. A separate sketch is made for each survey field. The sublot boundaries within the survey field are also surveyed. On the village map (using scales of about 1:4000 or 1:5000) only the survey field, not separate lots, is shown. After the map has been completed, the survey fields are numbered and the lots given sub-numbers. In a separate procedure the land is assessed and the tax determined. These records are kept in the revenue office. There is also a register authority for the registration of deeds.

Subdivisions are handled in different ways in different states. West Bengal, for example, has no administrative organization for maintaining records, and subdivisions are only surveyed in conjunction with general cadastral surveys, which are normally made at intervals of around 30 years. In other states, such as Andhra Pradesh and Tamil Nadu, there are special administrative offices which survey subdivisions and also keep registers with a record of changes. The problem of maintaining records is a difficult one. In addition, it is also felt that a register of titles, rather than a register of deeds, is needed.

The Torrens system has also had a great influence in western Canada. British Columbia, Alberta, Manitoba, Saskatchewan, and the Northwest Territories all have title registration systems following similar principles. In British Columbia and Manitoba, however, the old system of registration of deeds still exists alongside the system of title registration. In the eastern provinces, deed registration systems predominate, but the issue is under discussion. A law reform commission in Ontario (1971) recommended the introduction of a title registration system: 'Registration of titles is superior to registration of deeds in almost every material respect in which comparison can be made at present. A land titles system is also the system that can be best adapted to fit the needs of the future, particularly when seen as a major component of an integrated land information system.'

In the Maritime Provinces of eastern Canada a long-term project to create a parcel-based land information system was begun in the 1970s. The first stage was to establish and maintain a second-order control system; the next stage was to produce and maintain base maps and large-scale property maps to serve resource management, urban development, and parcel identification needs. This work is now nearly completed. The third stage, at present still being tested, is the conversion of the existing deeds system to a computerized guaranteed title registration system (Simpson 1984). A closer description is given in Appendix B.

5.4 Land registration in the United States

In the United States the legal land registration system is based mainly on private conveyance and the registration of deeds. Normally, the land units are surveyed. As authorized by Congress in 1785, the US Government proceeded to survey public lands within the framework of the rectangular system, dividing the land into quadrants one mile by one mile. Surveyed boundaries were marked or monumented on the ground. Corresponding field notes and plans were filed and maintained by the Department of the Interior. A cadastre was, however, never established. The system was not based on geodetic control or on an official plane co-ordinate system.

The principal motivation for creating a public registry of deeds was to encourage the transfer of titles in parcels of land from the public domain to private individuals, and to offer a measure of security in such titles. However, the record system did not always develop in a manner amenable to these needs. Scott (1981) describes the situation in the following way:

> During the earliest days of colonization, there was a clear understanding of the essential role of the 'Public Record' as a means of establishing the security of private interests in land holdings. Typically, two of the earliest acts of the new units of local government were the appointment of a Recording Clerk or Register of Deeds and an Official Surveyor or Deputy Surveyor-General. Original property boundary descriptions were prepared by the surveyor, and deeds and other agreements respecting the defined properties were placed in the Public Record for indexing and permanent public reference.
>
> Unfortunately, sufficient time and attention was not given to a full and proper documentation of these ownership records, so there was much that was done poorly or left undone entirely. Also, no attention was given to the many other aspects of a multipurpose land information system, so that the modern concept of such a system was not recognizable in these early records. Even the ever-present and all-important land taxation system was a somewhat later development, independently created

and, even to this day, functioning with the least possible amount of coordination between the tax office and the recorder's office ... In this manner, information about land was assembled in various unrelated offices and differing file structures. As the records grew in volume and complexity, the problem of gaining access to all needed information pertaining to specific parcels has become enormous.

There is now a firm consensus among both the public officers in charge and the many users of the public records, that traditional record keeping practices, which still predominate in most local governmental units, cannot meet current demands for ready access to complete information, and further that a major restructuring of the numerous indexing and filing systems is necessary and possible.

Serious attempts have been made to introduce title registration, but so far they have met only limited success. About 15 states have enacted Torrens statutes, but as title registration is voluntary and the primary costs of searching for and establishing title are high, registration is unusual.

Instead, title insurance is common. Private companies, each operating mainly within a single state, keep land records of their own. These are compiled and kept up to date by expert staff who make daily abstracts of pertinent details from the official records. Title insurance companies have thus duplicated and are maintaining public land records of entire communities and even entire counties in their own private title banks. The company can then insure a title if the records indicate that it is sound.

The companies' volume of business has increased dramatically in recent decades. By the year 1980 it had grown into an annual business of US$1.26 bn, according to Greulich (1983). He also points out that the companies retain not only the records but also the surveys.

The biggest drawback of title insurance surveys is their proprietary as well as their insular nature. In accordance with strict standards, the private land surveyor conducts very accurate field surveys of the land to be insured. Based on record research of relevant public boundaries and computation of field notes, a large scale (1:500 to 1:2000) boundary plan is then prepared. The registered land surveyor certifies to title insurer, owner, lessee and/or lender that the property boundaries as depicted on his plan are correct to the best of his professional ability [Fig.5.4]. Regrettably, the uncoordinated land parcel floats like an island among all other abutting, but unsurveyed, properties. There is usually no comprehensive large-scale cadastral map available, such as the Liegenschaftskarte in Germany or Switzerland, to which the title insurance survey can be related for permanent fit. The title insurance plan becomes the property of the private title insurance company, which will store it in its own data bank for its own future use. The abutting owners of such a survey are seldom aware of its existence.

The question of using all this material to develop a parcel-based land information system is under discussion in the USA, one reason being the need for better maps and records for tax purposes. During the 1970s, under the leadership of its Register of Deeds, Forsythe County set out to implement a very extensive modernization and integration of all land records in the county files, and to make provisions for adding a wide range of related data not previously included in any county record. A few years later, the North Caro-

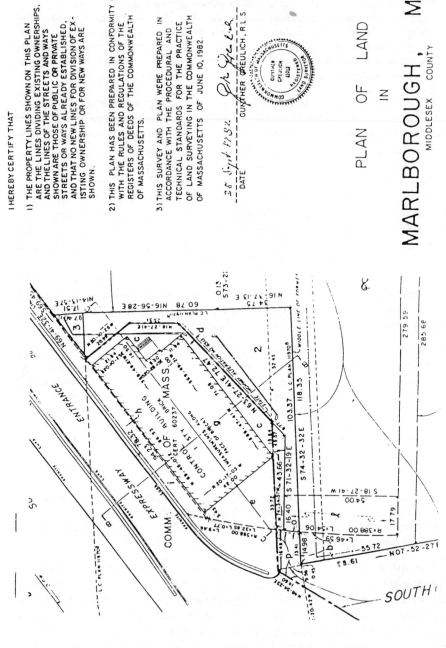

Fig. 5.4 Title insurance plan with certification by private land surveyor (from Greulich 1983)

lina Land Records Management programme was created by legislation providing for technical and financial assistance to qualifying counties. More recently, several states have placed greater emphasis upon integrated land records programmes, which draw together a truly comprehensive system with a unifying parcel identifier and a central index (Scott 1981).

An example is Wyandotte County, Kansas, which has developed a parcel-level, land records system. Principal components of the system are parcel maps on a scale of 1:1200, a comprehensive mainframe database of the characteristics of 66 000 parcels, and a topologically encoded file of digitized parcel boundaries. The system is operational and is maintained daily (Rhodes and Crane 1984). Another example is the system developed in Lane County, Oregon. All co-ordinates and data in the system are based on a single set of base maps and co-ordinate control. The parcel file includes all ownership and land use parcels in the county. Data attributes include tax map and parcel number, land use, number of residential living units, co-ordinates of the parcel perimeter and co-ordinates of the parcel centroid. The address file is a complete file of all site addresses, while the geocoded summary file includes all parcel file records with all commonly requested information geocoded, such as zoning, school attendance areas, census tracts, city limits, comprehensive plan designation, annexations, soils, flood plans, etc. It also includes tax valuation and appraisal information, such as the value of land and improvements (Swank 1983).

The National Research Council Panel on a Multipurpose Cadastre has studied the need, procedures and standards for such a cadastre and made recommendations (1980, 1982). According to Dueker *et al.* (1986) the NRC reports have helped to achieve a general consensus with respect to the following specific issues:

1. Establishment of a unique parcel numbering system

2. Development of a tract index

3. Assessment file content and need for standardized data definitions

4. Geodetic control and densification of monumentation

5. Base mapping procedure

6. Cadastral layer data structure

7. Spatially registered layers of other land data.

It is thus interesting to note that even if the Anglo-Saxon and the continental European countries have followed different roads concerning cadastre and legal land registers, their systems are often convergent. The former have never had cadastres, but there is a tendency to develop large-scale systematic maps showing parcel boundaries and linked to records, essentially centred on such technical data as parcel number, area, land use, and the co-ordinates of boundaries. Furthermore, the European cadastre tends to be more a description of property than an assessment record, while land registration, based on the cadastral units, has tended to approach a system of title registration. In both cases the cadastral maps and records are seen as essential for information systems based on identified land units. Automation and the development of computers have greatly expanded the potential for using units with unique designations as keys to the integration of different registers, and for linking all these data to geographical position. The basic need is the same, irrespective of historical and institutional development.

After this description of the general development in different countries we will more closely discuss the benefits of introducing or improving cadastral/land registration systems (Chs. 6 and 7) and then take up the question of feasibility studies (Ch. 8).

6

Benefits of cadastre and land register for development of rural and urban areas

Development of rural and urban areas is often seen as two independent processes. The problems are formulated in different ways: they are handled by different specialists and organizations using different methods. It may, therefore, be appropriate to start by underlining the fact that development of rural and urban areas is often closely interconnected and in many ways they have problems in common. The question of establishing a good cadastre and land register system should also be treated very much the same irrespective of rural or urban land. Often this is not done. Argumentation is built up from the one or the other side. But, none the less, the problems which cadastres and land registers are intended to solve are principally seen to be the same in rural and urban areas. This implies also that there should be the same laws, rules and methods concerning cadastre/land register for both types of land use.

In spite of this declaration, to avoid generalization it may be more appropriate to discuss rural and urban conditions separately.

6.1 Rural areas

No one can question the magnitude of the problem to develop the countryside and give a secure tenure for those working on land. To cite a World Bank seminar: 'At present, the livelihood of more than half of mankind depends directly on agriculture. Nine tenths of this total agricultural population is in developing countries, where questions of access and rights to land are of paramount interest to more than 2000 million people.'

It has often been pointed out that one strategic way to promote development is to strengthen the building of institutional structures. Cadastre and land register are weak sectors in most countries in the Third World. Strengthening these systems may, therefore, be a basic way to stimulate development.

In which ways can such an efficient system help?

1. Better information base for planning and administration.

2. Better specification of rights and more security.

3. Better possibilities to finance development.

4. Easier implementation of policy measures.

5. Better steering and control.

1. *Better information base for planning and administration* It is almost self-evident that to plan development of land one must know the basic facts concerning land. Some very basic facts are data about ownership structure and existing rights in the land in question. It is in most instances not sufficient to have a general knowledge on this point. Specific actions need specific knowledge. Detailed maps showing the parcel system are most valuable, especially if these maps have reference to a record, thus giving full evidence about rights in every parcel. Planning for irrigation and other infrastructural measures as well as running of schemes concerning seeds, fertilizer, credit, co-operation, etc., will all make great use of such information.

2. *Better specification of rights and more security* It is a well-known fact that especially in the Third World rights to land are often very obscure. Obvious examples are many countries in Africa. Traditionally customary rights to land have prevailed, more vested in the tribe, the group or the family than in the individual. In confrontation with Western rules introduced during the colonial period, commercialization, modern forms of cultivation, etc., there has been a tendency for the concept of individual rights to grow stronger and for the group rights to grow weaker. This can cause uncertainty about the actual situation and litigations concerning rights. Such development may have a negative effect on willingness to invest and develop. A land register can define the actual right and take away the uncertainty. There are also many other situations, where the right to land is ambiguous. Perhaps the land has been occupied. What right does a squatter have? Maybe the balance between public rights and individual rights to land is unclear. In such cases land registration may be of help.

Secure rights are important not only for farm land (see Fig. 6.1). As is well known, wood for fuel is scanty in great parts of the Third World. The natural regrowth is simply not sufficient. A great help would be if individual or village forests were planted on a large scale. But their growth takes many years. It must, therefore, be quite clear that the one who plants

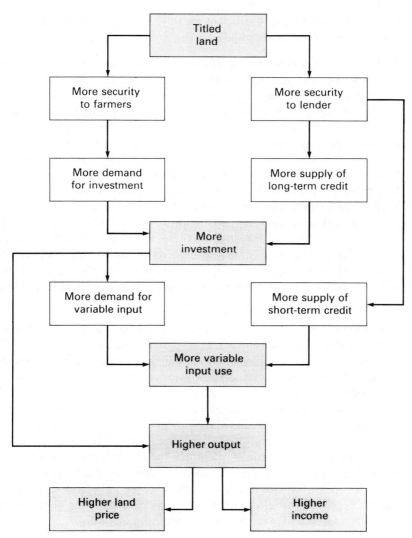

Fig. 6.1 Ownership security and farm planning (from Feder 1986)

them also has an exclusive right to cut them. This is obviously a problem in many parts of the world.

Sometimes the better specification of rights may have some negative social consequences. There may be a tendency to suppress rights which are lesser, or without legal support, or which are uncomfortable to the majority. Fixing of rights has in many cases resulted in restrictions on the extensive use of common land by smallholders. It also happens that lesser rights – widows' rights, etc. – are overlooked. Examples of these kinds were found when Kenya carried through an extensive land registration programme. Generally, however, security of title is especially important for the poor who have insufficient means to engage in protracted litigation concerning title and boundaries.

3. *Better possibilities to finance development*   The credit aspect is one of the main reasons for land registration. Most financial institutions insist on plans and good title before giving mortgages and loans, or they request special insurance to be taken. Development of the land, not least development of efficient and modern agriculture, often requires more resources than the owners command themselves or can borrow from co-operative societies – which normally provide only short-term credit – or from private money-lenders, who as a rule demand high rates of interest. Unless money is available at reasonable interest, it is seldom possible to finance considerable investments in land.

   This aspect may not seem so important in a rather simple society, where the tendency for investment is low, the credit possibilities in any case are limited because of general poverty in the society, and the land values seldom are high. But, as the country develops, the credit question will become increasingly important and some solutions must be reached, lest the development be seriously delayed.

4. *Easier action implementation*   As is well known, the most spectacular plans for development can turn into 'paper plans' which will never be realized. The normal difficulty to implement plans will increase greatly without detailed maps and good knowledge of existing ownerships and other rights in land.

   An obvious example is implementation of agrarian reforms. In this case, maps and records of land and rights in land are almost imperative. It has been the experience of several countries that, even when reform laws are enacted, it is very difficult to enforce them unless precise information about land tenure is available. Normally there is much opposition to overcome from big landowners. In the absence of a land register, the loopholes will often be too many, the implementation too slow and the difficulties too big to make the reform realistic.

5. *Better guidance and control*   The greater the knowledge of the land the better the possibilities will be to guide the development. If desired, special control mechanisms can be coupled into the land registration machinery. In many European countries – for example Sweden – subdivision of a parcel is allowed only after it has been reviewed by the appropriate public authority. Thus cadastre and land registration make it possible to control fragmentation, at least to a considerable degree. Also other types of control can be applied, for example that prescribed building improvement has taken place in case of a land grant, that transfers follow established rules, that prices do not exceed certain levels, etc.

   One reason for control may be the need to protect the farmer himself. This aspect has been emphasized in the Lawrance Mission report for Kenya (1966).

It was realised that freedom of disposition, though essential attribute of individual ownership, paradoxically must be withheld from the new owners in their own interest, if any account was to be taken of what had happened in India and Burma and other places where no control was exercised when individual ownership was first introduced into the native lands. Too often has it been proved, that there is no more certain way of depriving a peasant of his land than to give him a secure title and make it as readily negotiable as a bank note.

Partly for this reason, a system of land control was introduced in Kenya together with title registration. Transfers, leases, mortgages, partitions and subdivisions must have the consent of a Land Control Board before they become valid. If a transaction is markedly unfair to one of the parties, consent should be refused.

Because of the reasons mentioned it seems realistic to believe that cadastre and land registers together with supporting maps can be a vital tool to stimulate development. Experiences point in the same direction. Kenya, for example, is an outstanding country in the Third World in land registration. Since the 1960s most of the country has been covered by systematic registration of titles. During the same period a remarkable intensification of production has taken place, partly by expansion of intensive crops like coffee, partly by increased yields per hectare. According to a World Bank investigation (*The World Bank Research News* 7(1)), agricultural exports have tripled at a time when they have been static or diminished in other important African countries. Much the same has happened in Malawi, another country with secure ownerships (see Fig. 6.2). It is always difficult to determine the principal reasons behind such a change, but it seems not unrealistic to believe that the secure ownership after registration in combination with better credit possibilities and extensive agricultural advice activity have played a considerable part in these production increases.

On the other hand, it must be remembered that a cadastral and land registration system is not a magic tool *per se*, which more or less automatically induces development. It is a part of institutional development and must be combined with other measures to give real results. To cite some words of J. Lawrance (1984):

The discussion suggests that some of the claims more commonly made in favour of land registration as an agent of agricultural productivity are often overstated or based on misconceptions. They certainly warrant more critical examination than is usually accorded to them. Over-enthusiastic claims may well weaken the case. The conclusion is:
(a) The introduction of land registration does not contribute automatically or directly to agricultural productivity, for it does not necessarily alter the nature, use or tenure of the land. Nor does it change the attitudes or practices of the farmers on whom productivity depends.
(b) Other inputs are always necessary to effect these changes.

(c) Land registration can, however, facilitate or complement these other inputs in various ways, and this contribution to productivity is valuable.

6.2 Urban areas

In a World Bank study by Doeble (1985) we read:

Urban land is among the most valuable economic and social resources of any nation, and it cannot be properly managed without an adequate system for the measurement and recording of the boundaries of parcels, and the registration of all legal rights related to each parcel, that is to say, without an adequate cadastral system. At a time when land is becoming an increasingly difficult and time consuming element in virtually every development project, the lack of cadastral information has become ever more critical. However, it is in precisely those countries in which the rate of urbanization in the next two decades is expected to be most rapid that cadastral systems tend to be weakest. The establishment of such systems is therefore now becoming regarded as much a part of basic infrastructure as roads and electric grids: an essential element to expedite virtually all other forms of development.

and he continues:

50% of all World Bank urban projects between 1972 and 1982 have encountered additional costs and/or substantial delays due to inadequate cadastral and property tax systems.

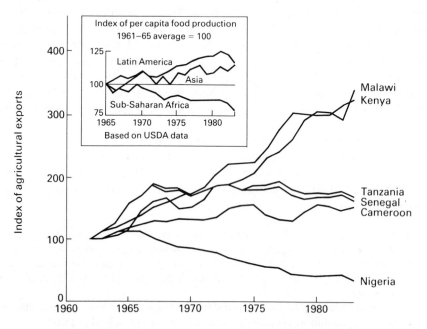

Three-year moving averages using 1984 average prices

Fig. 6.2   Index of agricultural exports in some African countries (from The World Bank 1986)

The main goal for urban development can be formulated as follows: 'The provision of secure tenure for land in adequate quantities, in suitable locations at affordable prices and on equitable terms is a fundamental requirement for clearing the backlog of housing demand for the poor and meeting the rapidly growing need to house new poor families', (HABITAT: Guidelines for the preparation of shelter programmes, Nairobi 1984).

This backlog is enormous, mainly because of the urban explosion in the Third World. During the last 25 years a large number of monstrous cities have developed. The trend is continuous. In the last two decades of the twentieth century the urban population may be more than twice as large as before. And, what is still more serious, most of the new habitations will be irregular, outside the public planning sector and often slum.

How to fight against such a situation? What are the strategic problems? To increase planning and building as such is, of course, important. But the underlying problem is most often land: its availability, prices and security of rights to land.

During the 1950s and 1960s the accepted solution to diminish slums and solve the shelter problems was to bulldoze slum areas and build new houses for rental. It was a form of action borrowed from the more developed industrial world. However, it was gradually realized that it did not work as the main solution in the Third World. The dwellings produced were far too expensive for most of the poor, and the economies of developing countries can hardly afford any subsidies.

Instead, the prevailing idea nowadays is to rely on self-activity. Many, perhaps most, of those living in slum areas have a surplus of time not spent in gainful employment. This surplus can then be used for building, if land is provided and a right to stay on the land is secured.

Normally two ways are recommended to solve the immediate housing problems of large population masses.

The first way – the provision of *sites and services* – normally involves low cost exploitation of unused areas owned, controlled or bought by the government or a municipality. A simple infrastructure of dirt roads, standpipes and public facilities serves a regular system of small sites. Right of ownership or occupancy is given if a dwelling of certain standard is built within a given time period. Sometimes public help is provided for building the shell of the house, often in terms of loans for building material. But to achieve low costs, most of the construction must be left to self-activity.

The other way – the *upgrading of squatter areas* – means that irregular dwellings without any formal right to the land are tolerated and in fact looked upon as a resource. Some houses are pulled down in order to make room for a road system. But essentially the buildings are retained and a simple infrastructure is provided. And, most important, the dwellers are given the right to stay and a formal right to land ownership or occupancy for a prescribed time. This means that they can confidently improve the standard of their houses and their living conditions successively.

In both these solutions, the cadastre and land registers play a central role. It is obvious that there must be some means to give the dweller *security*, some formal document which defines his right to the plot, otherwise the self-activity will be very much hampered. This purpose can be achieved even with simple systems. It has, for example, been proposed in some World Bank projects to just number the houses on aerial pictures of squatter areas and then give these identified dwellers, who are allowed to stay, a formal document of right to occupancy for a certain time period. This may work well as a temporary solution. In the long run it is advisable to use a system with more permanent registration routines.

So the security aspect is as vital in urban as in rural areas. Also the other reasons for the cadastre and land register are much the same. It is obvious that they have great use from an *information and planning* aspect. Every planner needs to know what land resources are available. Which land is still not used for infrastructure or for buildings – planned or irregular? How suitable is it for different urban purposes? Who owns or controls this land? Without such basic information, planning of the urban development will be difficult.

In industrialized society, a parcel-based land information system can be built up in a more sophisticated way. Digitized maps and automated and integrated registers can render many services for the planner. Maps in different scales and in different combinations of overlays and content can easily be produced. If the basic information concerning land, use, population, buildings and enterprises has a common identifier in the uniquely determined parcel, integrated information in the form of statistics, thematic maps, etc., can be produced. Even in the most developed countries we have only started to take stock of all the possibilities which a computer-based land information system can open for the planner.

An important feature of such a system is that it makes updating easier. Up to now much of the planner's work has consisted of taking inventories and bringing forward information needed for a special plan. If, after some years, the plan were to be revised, the inventory work had to start anew. It is a difficult and inefficient way to work. Operation control, monitoring and revision of goals and plans will be much improved if the planner always can communicate with updated relevant land databases in his work.

The other main advantages mentioned for rural areas: better financing possibilities, easier action implementation and better guidance and control are equally relevant for urban areas. Without a secure title, it is difficult to obtain *credit* for building. When the standard is very low there is, of course, both low availability and low need for bank credit. In order to raise the standard or to build in a good standard from the start, such credit is a must in most cases. Public *action implementation* of different kinds is well facilitated if there is a cadastre or land register covering the area. For taxes it is self-evident. But the register is also useful in many other ways. Lists of land, of landowners and of people living on the land are needed for many purposes: census, elections, land and population statistics, etc. Public administration is difficult without basic knowledge in these respects.

Better *guidance and control* are immensely important in preventing the urban explosion in the Third World from destroying the total structure. As mentioned earlier, new habitations in those countries are to a great part unplanned, irregular and often slums. If a regulating system is ever to function, there is a need not only for knowledge about existing rights and people but also for some legal means to influence the development. In a title registration system these are naturally applied in registration as such. Without registration, irregular building is difficult to prevent. All formal physical plans will then have a tendency to be no more than paper plans.

So, cadastre and land registration are in many respects vital for urban development. But they are not sufficient. They are only a component of the infrastructural and institutional framework, which must be built to get development under control and to guide it in the right direction. Land at affordable prices must be made available, by public acquisition or in other ways, the legal base for land use and tenure must be strengthened, the land management and financial systems must be improved, the norms for building standards to get building permission must be adapted to the economic resources of ordinary people, the role of local authorities should be revised, public participation must be strengthened, etc. An efficient system of land registration is certainly not sufficient as a single measure.

I, therefore, would like to emphasize the words of Simpson (1976):

> Land registration must be kept in perspective. It is a device which may be essential to sound land administration, but it is merely part of the machinery of government. It is not some sort of magical specific which will automatically produce good land use and development; nor is it a system of land holding (land tenure), it is not even a kind of land reform, though it may be a valuable administrative aid to land reform. In short, land registration is only a means to an end. It is not an end in itself.

7

Further benefits of cadastral and land registration systems. Calculating benefits

In the previous chapter, it was argued that cadastral/land registration systems have several positive features which should enable them to play a strategic role in rural and urban development. In this chapter we will discuss some other benefits of the systems.

7.1 Improved basis for land assessment and taxation

As mentioned in other contexts, one of the prime objects of a cadastre is to provide a better basis for land taxation. Historically, taxation has often taken place on the basis of very crude, simple records or without any records at all. But a good cadastral system, based on maps and embodying the unique identification of each land unit, provides several benefits.

It *increases revenues* by making taxation coverage complete. Experiences from many countries indicate that without fully inclusive records, tax collection will be incomplete, resulting in considerable losses in public revenues.

It can produce *a fairer system*. Without sufficient knowledge of the boundaries and acreage of each land unit, it is impossible to determine fair land taxes. Instead, schematic assessment becomes necessary, making tax charges more arbitrary. This also increases the risk of corruption.

The taxation system will be *more efficient*. Pervasive failure to pay diminishes the fairness of the taxation system. Proper records of land units and their responsible owners facilitate tax collection, and make it easier to verify payment. Improved efficiency can substantially reduce costs and frustration.

A good land taxation system may have many advantages in addition to giving the government more revenue. If some of the revenue is retained locally, it will augment the effectiveness of the local authorities and institutions. Local authorities often obtain most of their revenue from land taxes.

These can, therefore, became a powerful instrument to decentralize administration, strengthen local authorities and provide means for local development. The money could be used to defray the cost of roads, sewers, water pipes and other utilities, and to establish funds for maintenance and further improvements. Taxes can also be used to stimulate development in other ways. If the assessment is made according to potential rather than actual land use, it becomes too expensive to let the land lie idle, and development and structural improvements tend to increase.

It is true that land taxation and other land charges are often very incomplete today – especially in the Third World. It may sometimes be argued that because of this, the benefits of a cadastral system are small. But since land is a major resource, it is quite natural that it be included in a revenue system – in one way or the other. In the long run a cadastre/land register will considerably facilitate the development of a modern, well-adapted land taxation system.

7.2 Administrative benefits

Cadastres and land registers can serve administration in many ways in addition to contributing to a comprehensive, equitable and efficient land tax system. It has already been mentioned that the unique identification of the land units can be used for other records such as population data, etc. It is easy to see how comprehensive information linked to convenient units of land can be most useful for planning and administration of all kinds, including necessary communications between authorities and citizens. Local administrations especially can be strengthened in this way, but even central and regional administrations involved in land planning, development and management can benefit greatly from such systems.

These arguments are largely self-explanatory, and only one aspect will be elaborated here. It is common practice in many countries to establish special records for the activities of a specific department or a specific sector, without giving sufficient consideration to the fact that some of the data may also be of interest to other departments and sectors. If joint effort were made to establish a multipurpose information system involving different sectors of the society, the system would be more productive, and there would be less duplication of effort. In another context, I have studied the land information structure in two Third World countries and found much duplication. Separate registers were established for agricultural support and credit, tenure control, control of agricultural products and commodities, agricultural census, population census, social security, parliamentary elections, assessment and taxes, registration of deeds, etc. The records were seldom co-ordinated, and different units were used. The information was mainly collected within a specific sector and for a single purpose, resulting in much duplication. With a comprehensive system of cadastres and land registration, such a problem can largely be avoided. Every department and sector involved can contribute its own specific information, and be responsible for keeping the information up to date. If the information is communicated or open to other sectors, duplication of effort will be radically diminished, and the administration will be more effective.

7.3 Improving map production

Good maps are highly important for a country. Especially in the Third World countries, planning and development are often complicated and delayed because of the lack of good maps. The shortage of detailed, large-scale maps is especially evident in connection with development planning, water projects and so on.

A most useful by-product of a cadastre or land register is the register map, which is usually in a scale larger than 1:10000. Experience shows that when such a map is available, it will soon be used for a variety of purposes – in administration, for all kinds of land projects and for private use. A register map can be an especially valuable and flexible tool if it is digitized and includes different kinds of information in overlays. It is then easy to vary the scale and content of the map. Studies made in industrialized countries indicate that the demand for different products would be so strong, that the benefits of the digitized map would often exceed the costs several times over (Bernhardsen and Tveitdal, 1987).

The time aspect is important in this connection. It is very advantageous if good maps are available before planning and development are begun. If no large-scale map exists, it may, of course, be produced expressly for the planning and development in question. But this will often take considerable time, not least in developing countries with meagre resources. There is an obvious risk that, in the absence of maps, all planning and other enterprises will be greatly delayed, or even come to a complete halt because of heavy surveying costs. The total amount of planning and investment will decrease in a society without suitable maps.

7.4 Less litigation and less work for the courts

In a society with gradually changing attitudes towards group or individual ownership/occupancy – as is often the case when a market economy makes inroads in a customary society – there are bound to be conflicts and litigation concerning land. The same is true in situations where squatting and irregular, or even illegal, occupations are common. The result is disputes and interpersonal problems within the private sector as well as conflicts between individuals and the public interest. It also means abundant work for the courts. Especially in the Third World, a great percentage of court cases concern land. The entire society has, therefore, much to gain by clarifying boundaries and rights in land. Undoubtedly, the best way to do so is by establishing an efficient and comprehensive system of land registration. It can practically eliminate all uncertainty concerning the extent and content of rights in land. The essence of such a system is to define both the concepts of different rights and their objects.

7.5 Easier transactions in land

Without reliable land registers, transactions in land will often be costly, time consuming and uncertain. It is normally necessary to establish the fact that the reputed owner or trustee actually has the legal right to deal with the property. This is sometimes a rather complicated process, and in many countries which lack a register of titles, it is, therefore, common practice to use legal experts for searches and establishment of title. The costs are often substantial. Another model – used frequently in the USA as mentioned above – is to insure title, which, of course, can also be expensive. A land register which provides guaranteed information on all existing rights in land not only makes searches unnecessary, but also makes it possible to use simpler forms of conveyance. In this way the need for expensive legal assistance can be greatly reduced.

7.6 Establishing a land market

One difficulty facing many developing countries is the absence of a real land market. The reasons may be unclear delimitation of individual and group rights, insecure ownership and so on. A title registration system can remove such obstacles. The necessity for a functioning land market will become increasingly apparent the more the society is transformed into a market economy. It makes it easier to bring about appropriate land uses, and will facilitate the establishment of efficient and consistent land policies – not least in the urban sector. A smoothly functioning land market opens the way not only for private development but also for public land acquisition and other means of ensuring that land is available for dwellings and other urban needs.

Many points concerning the benefits of cadastres and land registers could be developed further. Some have already been mentioned in other contexts. The relative importance of different benefits varies considerably depending on local conditions. Their relevance must always be studied in the context of the country or the region in question. It must also be kept in mind that the introduction of a cadastral/land registration system will not automatically provide all the benefits discussed here. The full effect can only be achieved when such a system is combined with other appropriate measures.

Before leaving the discussion of benefits, some issues concerning cost-benefit calculations will be dealt with.

7.7 Calculating benefits

The introduction of cadastral and land registration systems, or major changes in such systems, will entail substantial costs irrespective of which methods are chosen. As always, decisions concerning such heavy investments should not be taken without attempting to work out the relationship between benefits and costs. Most likely, the officials responsible for the decision will demand some sort of economic feasibility study as well.

It is, however, quite obvious that many of the advantages are very difficult to express in monetary terms. If, for example, some kind of cadastre/land register makes possible agrarian reform, what is this worth in money? Or is it possible to determine the monetary value of better control of urban development?

We must, therefore, accept the fact that it is hardly possible to demonstrate all the benefits of an improved cadastral/land registration system monetarily. To a great extent, it is a tool for strengthening institutional structures, and making it easier for the public to implement a chosen policy. This does not, however, remove the obligation to demonstrate the gains of the improved system as far as is possible.

One way is to refer to empirical evidences. Thus according to Feder (1987) a comparison in some provinces in rural Thailand between the values of titled and untitled land showed that the former normally were higher than the values of the untitled land, mostly considerably higher.

Such investigations can give a certain general knowledge. However, estimates are also needed of the benefits in the special case.

What then can be done?

The first task is to *specify the current situation*, to define the starting point. What is the existing system, how does it work, and what are its shortcomings. Further, it is necessary to *define the proposed new system or alternative systems*. The more precisely the existing and proposed systems are described, the easier it will be to evaluate the effects of the changes.

The next step should be to *express the benefits* in verbal terms. This implies a discussion similar to Chapter 6 and Sections 7.1–7.6. But before a specific benefit is added to the list, it must be carefully considered whether it is really valid in the context of the country or region in question. If this is not done, the list will merely be an uninteresting rehash of general writings on cadastres/land registration.

When the list is finished, an attempt should be made to *evaluate* the benefits one by one. To begin with, this will be in general terms such as weak, moderate, strong, or unimportant, noteworthy, considerable, very substantial. If possible it should also be noted whether the benefit in question is mainly private or public in nature. Even if the results are not expressed in figures, such a presentation will still afford a thorough analysis of the situation, and will also provide much information for the decision-makers.

In many cases and in many countries, it is difficult to come much further than this – especially in developing countries with weak documentation and statistics. But, if possible, some important terms should be expressed in monetary values.

Some examples will be given. One important effect in the private sector may be that an efficient land register could possibly eliminate the need for title searches in land transactions, and maybe even for legal help. Perhaps it is possible to make a fair estimate of the normal cost of legal assistance for an average transaction. With knowledge of the number of transactions in round figures, a crude estimate can be made of the monetary value of this benefit. An example of calculation of costs for different alternative methods used in the USA is given by Janczyk (1979).

It may also be possible to find out how much of the courts' time is devoted to land cases nationally or in a certain region. A rough estimate could then be made of the expected reduction in the amount of cases, and of what this would mean in terms of costs.

One important benefit may be increased revenues in the form of taxes, ground rent or charges for utilities, etc. This is due to more comprehensive records of those liable for rents and taxes, to improved verification of payment and to a better basis on which to estimate taxes, etc. Good land records may also be a prerequisite for introducing a system of land taxes or ground rents. Pilot studies in selected test areas may help to estimate how much revenues can be expected to increase with the introduction of a cadastral and land registration system. This increase is a benefit for the government or the local authorities rather than for society as a whole. Nevertheless, better land records may have a potentially very substantial effect, perhaps of the same magnitude as the total costs for the new system. A calculation of the monetary value of such benefits may, therefore, be a very convincing argument when the government is deciding about land records.

Another benefit, which it may be possible to estimate in monetary terms, is the decrease in administrative costs. A joint information base concerning land will not only facilitate land management and communications between authorities and citizens, it will also greatly reduce duplication of effort as discussed above. Even if it is difficult to obtain precise figures on what this implies in terms of cost reduction, a study of the present routines in the more important departments and authorities involved may provide basic material for determining the magnitude of the potential savings.

As mentioned earlier, cadastral maps are useful in many connections in addition to cadastres and land registers. Interviews and questionnaires answered by major users can provide information about the purposes for which the maps are used, the frequency and the benefits. Such studies might indicate that large-scale maps of the cadastral type are economical even without the introduction of an improved cadastral/land registration system. If so the costs of map production could be excluded in the comparison between the benefits and costs of the proposed system.

A very important question for the determination of the benefit/cost ratio is the effect on production. Will agricultural production increase because of improved security, greater willingness to invest, better credit opportunities, etc. If so, what is a fair assumption concerning a probable percentage increase? What will this mean in terms of increased national income? What costs, in addition to the direct costs for cadastres/land registration, are necessary to reach this goal? What does the expected increase in urban, owner-built homes mean in combination with the improved credit opportunities and what is the monetary value of these developments? Obviously, these are very difficult questions. But even a very crude estimate of production benefits may have a decisive effect on the result of the calculations.

Admittedly, it will never be possible to evaluate all the benefits in monetary terms, and most estimates will be uncertain. Even so, it is recommended that calculations of some kind be undertaken. They may not always be decisive, but they are a way of systematizing the study of probable benefits in the case in point, and of obtaining better understanding of the effects of introducing or improving a cadastral/land registration system.

There is one factor which may simplify estimates of the benefit/cost ratio. A cadastral/land registration system can be introduced successively. It is true that the system must be complete and comprehensive to have full effect – but this can be on a regional, rather than a national, basis. Systematic registration, by its very nature, implies that the system is extended gradually, and that, consequently, it can be adopted region by region. A good example is England, where the original decision to introduce a title registration system did not concern the whole country, but only a few specified regions. This means that benefit/cost calculations need only cover the regions in question and not the whole country. It also means that feasibility studies can normally be concentrated on the most favourable parts of the country, where the benefits can be expected to be high or the costs low. Even rough calculations will usually be sufficient to show that the introduction or improvement of cadastres/land registers would be economical in these cases, if suitable standards are chosen and the costs are carefully considered. If these regions are large enough, the systems can be given legal and institutional backing and introduced there. Decisions concerning possible extension can be deferred to the future when more experience about actual benefits and costs will be available.

The benefit/cost discussion will normally be part of the feasibility studies, and Chapter 8 discusses these studies in more detail.

8

Feasibility studies for establishing or improving a cadastral and land registration system

Prior to taking any decision on a cadastral/land registration system, a *feasibility study* should be conducted. The principal stages in such a study are presented in this chapter as follows:

- Investigation and presentation of basic facts
- Analysis of existing problems and of the possible benefits of major changes
- Pilot studies
- Cost estimates
- Definition of principal goals
- Choice of principal methods
- Choice of priorities and areas
- Definition of legal measures.

8.1 Investigation and presentation of basic facts

As in any study, investigations of existing conditions should concentrate on basic features of special importance. Major categories in this connection are usually:

- existing land records and maps;
- existing tenure and legal structure; and
- available resources.

It goes without saying that the *existence, content and status of land records and maps* are of fundamental importance when deciding about new or improved systems. To what extent do records of the cadastral or land register type exist within the country? Are such records only sporadic, or do they provide more-or-less complete coverage of the land within certain regions or within the country as a whole? Do they include both private and public land? Are they based on identified and unique land units? In what way are changes in these units recorded, and how are the records maintained? What kind of organization is responsible? For what purposes are the records used, and what information do they provide concerning location, boundaries, areas, land uses, values, taxes, etc.? What status do they have? For example, are land registers of the deed or title type? To what extent are land records of different types based on large-scale maps on which the land units can be identified? Are there any other maps which might be useful for the purpose? Are geodetic control net, modern aerial photographs, etc., available? These are some basic facts which have to be documented as a basis for the following analysis.

It is also essential to investigate the *existing tenure structure*. For example, it is important when designing the registration system to know whether individual ownership or group-oriented, customary rights are predominant. If the latter is the case, this would not prevent land registration, but other kinds of definitions of rights would have to be considered. The prevalence of illegal occupation, squatting, etc., would indicate registration problems, which would have to be resolved in one way or another. If the tenure situation includes ownership as well as long-term occupancy rights or leases, decisions would have to be taken about how to handle these different forms of tenure. If tenure is highly fragmented, this would influence the costs as well as the final benefits of cadastral and land registration activities. In such cases, there is reason to combine registration with land consolidation measures. The frequency of co-ownership may also be important. Since tenure problems are heavily influenced by the *legal situation* in general, this area must also be studied thoroughly. We will return to this matter in the last section of the chapter.

It is not unusual for the conditions mentioned above to vary from region to region within a country. Cadastres and land registration may exist in some major towns but not in the countryside. Or there may be areas where written law prevails, and others where customary law is in effect. Such regional differences within a country must be clarified.

Knowing which *resources are available to implement the task* is also of importance for decisions concerning new systems. Availability means that the resources can be reckoned with on a long-term basis since both cadastres and land registers are long-term projects. This presupposes lasting political support and national economic conditions and technical standards which make the implementation of a project of this kind appear feasible. If the necessary know-how, personnel and equipment are not available, it must be possible to make up these deficiencies through foreign support, additional allowances and/or expanded educational programmes. If decisions about new systems are taken before the matter of resources is resolved, areas to be included must be chosen with great selectivity.

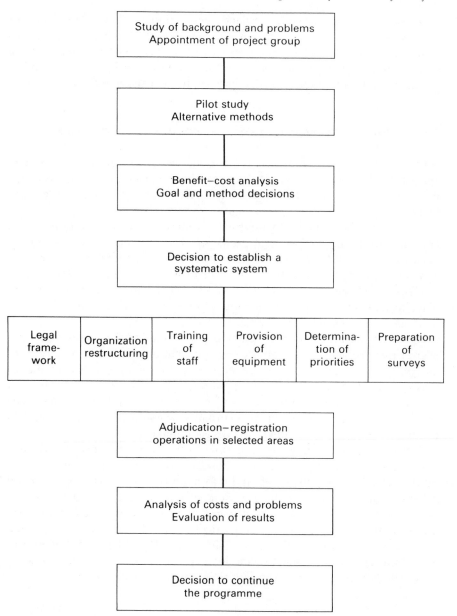

Fig. 8.1 Introduction of systematic registration

Other circumstances may be of interest as well. For example, since an important aspect of land registration is that it stimulates bank loans, knowledge about the supply and demand of such credits is an essential prerequisite for estimating the benefits of a new system. The frequency of land litigation and the need for legal advice for land transactions, etc., may, as emphasized earlier, be other factors pertinent to the potential benefits of a new system.

Decisions concerning cadastres/land registration are highly political, not only because of the long-term costs involved, but also because measures concerning land are politically sensitive. The basic factors influencing a decision must, therefore, be presented in a way which is clear and understandable, not only to the specialist but also to the general public.

8.2 Analysis of existing problems and benefits of a new or improved system

Where there are no problems, there is no need for reform. A problem analysis is the basis for decisions concerning changes in existing systems. Problem analysis must, therefore, be assigned a prominent place in a feasibility study.

Very often the impulse to improve a cadastral/land registration system emanates from one or two main problems. The problems may concern the need for a fairer land taxation system, insecurity of ownership, the unavailability of banking credits with falling investment rates as a result, the need to implement agrarian reforms or other structural changes, the lack of adequate planning and management information systems or difficulties in implementing plans and guiding urban development.

However, even if the impulse emanates from one particular problem, and even if this problem appears to be the principal one, it is still important to analyse the total picture. A comprehensive analysis often reveals a number of reasons for reforming the existing situation, and the need for a change may then appear far more economical and convincing. Ample time and space should, therefore, be devoted to a broad discussion of problems, and to making a concise presentation to the decision-makers.

Problem identification is also the basis for assessing benefits. As was discussed earlier, it is seldom possible to make comprehensive, formal calculations concerning the benefits of land information systems. Making a general list of common benefits is not sufficient in this context. To have any real value, the study must try to present a fair estimate of the impact of a reform given the special conditions of the particular area. In order to convince the government, it will probably be necessary not only to identify problems but also to present some formal, schematic calculations for some major items, to show whether the gains are sufficient to justify the calculated costs.

8.3 Pilot studies

Some pilot studies must normally be carried out in the field in the course of a feasibility study. They may have various objectives:

- To get a better picture of tenure and property structure.

- To test different methods of communication and co-operation between authorities and owner-occupiers in an area.

- To test different survey methods.

- To get some idea of the costs.

In developing countries and especially in customary lands, there is usually a dearth of statistics, and sometimes even of detailed knowledge, about tenure conditions such as owner–tenant relations, the frequency of co-ownership, the degree of fragmentation, etc. A few case studies cannot provide reliable statistics, but they can give some idea of conditions normally encountered in such areas.

It is crucial for the establishment of a cadastral/land registration system that information concerning the operation reaches the proper owner-occupiers, that they are aware of its purpose and the necessity of making their claims, and that they are willing to co-operate. Pilot studies can suggest some suitable methods for achieving these ends, and thus be of importance for the design of the final operational system.

One crucial question concerning survey methods is whether or not photogrammetry and interpretation of aerial photographs can be used extensively. To a great extent it is a question of whether there are defined boundaries on the ground and, if so, whether they are visible from the air. Pilot studies of typical areas can give some ideas of the possibilities and thus a better base for estimates concerning methods and feasibility of the project.

Generally, pilot studies also give a base for estimates of the amount of time required and resources available. By comparing this information with conceptions within the survey organization, etc., of the amount of time normally required for different tasks, it is possible to obtain an approximate idea of the resources needed for implementing a planned programme.

It is advantageous, if enough pilot areas can be studied, to include areas with serious problems as well as typical areas. Normally, however, this is not possible because of the costs. The few pilot studies may, therefore, concentrate on areas, which in one way or another, typify conditions in larger regions.

8.4 Cost estimates

Normally, a feasibility study should also include cost estimates. This is not easy in the case of establishing cadastre/land register. Unlike what applies to most other investments, there is mostly little or no experience of such operations within a developing country. Cost figures from other countries should be used with great care because of differences in institutional organization, methods employed and the general wage situation.

Some relationships between different cost categories may, however, be of more general interest. One such rule of thumb is that survey and demarcation costs tend to be far and away the greatest component of total expenditures. The relative costs of the process were estimated in an example provided by Howells (1974) from some Caribbean islands where adjudication of title is combined with simple methods of parcel survey. According to this example, administrative overheads (including training and supervision) accounted for some 12 per cent, demarcation 28 per cent, recording 14 per cent, survey 40 per cent and the adjudication of disputes and petitions 6 per cent of the total costs. Lawrance (1985) concludes: 'Demarcation and survey will often account for a substantial part of the total cost, perhaps as much as 75%'. Cost estimates should, therefore, concentrate especially on these items.

As will be discussed in a later chapter, cadastral surveys and demarcation can be performed using widely differing methods, and with great variations in costs. It is, therefore, not possible to present any general figures about absolute costs. In most countries, however, there are rules of thumb available concerning time, resources and costs required by different types of surveying operations. Records from pilot studies may also help. It is true, however, that cost estimates in this field are often difficult and uncertain. As Dale (1976) comments: 'When tenders are submitted for mapping by commercial survey companies, there is always a wide variation in the prices quoted, with costs, at times, varying by a factor of 4 for the same contract.'

Moreover, costs are not dependent only on survey methods. The scale of operations is also a decisive factor. Generally the costs per land unit are very much higher in sporadic surveys of single land units than in systematic surveys of large areas. In the latter case, sophisticated methods such as photogrammetric techniques may be used, transport costs will be lower per unit, etc. These matters will be discussed in more detail later.

8.5 Definition of principal goals

After the background and problems of existing systems have been investigated, and the potential benefits and costs of alternative, new or improved systems have been calculated, it is time to decide on which principal goals to base the system. Three main goals can be discussed:

1. To use the system mainly for general land information.
2. To use the system for certain administrative purposes as well, such as tax determination and collection, etc.
3. To establish a multipurpose cadastral/land registration system.

Using the system mainly for general land information

A land information system can be structured in different ways depending on the kind of information wanted. For environmental data, for example, ecologically homogeneous areas may be appropriate. The subdivision may be fine or coarse depending on the problems. A linear structure based on existing roads, streets and other communications infrastructure may be preferable for data on traffic or communications. For many types of land data, however, the most suitable information base may, as earlier stressed, be obtained by subdividing large statistical or administrative areas into smaller sub-units such as parcels or groups of parcels belonging to the same ownership/occupancy unit.

In its simplest form, such a system is merely a record of existing land units. Historically, this has usually been the first step. These records have often been very useful even without the support of any map. In Sweden, for example, such lists of taxable units were used not only for tax collection, but also for land registration purposes, gathering of population data, etc. The problem is the unique identification key. To a certain extent, this problem can be solved by grouping the units into villages or other pre-defined blocks, and then differentiating among them by means of owners' names, tax liability, description of the boundaries, etc. To serve as basic units in a general land information system, however, they must be distinctly identifiable. The best way to achieve this is by means of a map with numbered land units.

Such a map can be prepared to some extent by compiling existing surveys. In developing countries with a short surveying history, such material is often insufficient, and new systematic surveys are required. For general information purposes, a high degree of survey accuracy is unnecessary. Aerial photographs can be used for the most part. However, in many areas, existing boundaries are not easily discernible from the air, and a great deal of field work will be necessary. Due to these considerable costs, a pure information system is seldom economical if it cannot also be used for other purposes. Goal 1 is, therefore, usually not appropriate, unless the costs can be kept on a very moderate level. We should instead consider goals 2 or 3.

Using the system for specific administrative purposes as well

A typical purpose is taxation and tax collection, that is, the principal justification for the classical cadastre. This may be a valid justification in countries where land tax is an important source of income for the local community or the state. A good cadastral system can increase revenues substantially, and also make taxation fairer. If such a system exists it can also be used to satisfy other types of administrative needs. For tax collection, the initial ownership lists need not be very accurate. If anyone is wrongly made liable to pay taxes, he can appeal and the list will be corrected. The maps, on the other hand, are used for assessment, area determination, etc., and have to be reasonably accurate. The establishment of a comprehensive cadastral system will, therefore, involve considerable costs and resources. The question is whether this is reasonable and economically feasible. Can certain improvements be made, which will greatly increase its usefulness? This brings us to a discussion of goal 3.

A multipurpose cadastral/land registration system

In previous chapters, we have discussed the benefits of cadastral/land registration systems. These discussions showed that many of the benefits could only be realized when a cadastral system was combined with a reliable land registration system. The UN Ad Hoc Group of Experts on Cadastral Surveying and Mapping (1973), therefore, strongly recommended that if a cadastral system were to be established, it should be in combination with a 'legal' cadastre, that is, a legal land register preferably of the title registration type. While the costs would only be slightly higher, the benefits would be much greater. They argued as follows:

> The determination of boundaries and rights for legal purposes may be a slower, and so more costly, process than the determination of boundaries and owners or users for fiscal purposes, but often only marginally so. It is clearly wasteful to record owners or users when, with a little more effort, all legal rights in the parcel could be ascertained at the same time. Moreover if the legal rights are not determined, appreciable losses to individuals and the State will continue to occur until an efficient legal cadastre is established.

If special circumstances do not indicate otherwise, the general goal when establishing or improving a cadastral system should be to include title registration. This means:

- a clear definition of each parcel of land within a given area. Ideally, the parcels are defined on maps;
- a legal ascertainment of rights in land, and a special entry for each land unit, where these rights are registered;
- a public guarantee of the registered rights, or at least a very strong legal position for all inscribed rights;
- continued maintenance of the register and the maps including the obligation to register all land transactions and subdivisions.

Such a cadastral/land registration system should be designed to serve as a sound basis for a more fully developed land information system in the future. This means that it must be possible to use the land unit or other items in the cadastre as 'keys' for accessing other records. Furthermore, the information provided in cadastres/land registers should be concentrated so as to facilitate both maintenance and automation.

8.6 Choice of principal methods

Essentially, three main methods may be used to establish a title registration system (see Fig. 8.2):

1. Voluntary (sporadic) registration upon application of a landowner.
2. Compulsory (sporadic) registration whenever land is sold or given by grant or partitioned by legal process.
3. Compulsory (systematic) registration of all land (possibly with some exceptions) supported by cadastral surveys carried out area by area.

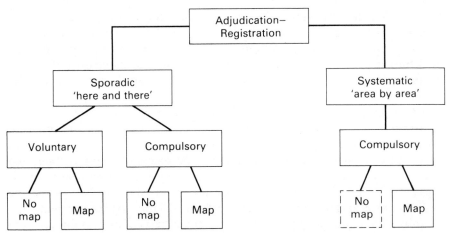

Fig. 8.2 Main methods of title registration. Sporadic registration is sometimes implemented without new surveys – this seldom happens in the case of systematic
registration

If system 1 is used, it is easy to start registration, and it is possible, furthermore, to have the landowner or the applicant bear the costs. The system is,
therefore, widely used, especially in Third World countries. But all experience has shown that it will take a very long time before any appreciable
amount of land is registered. The costs per registered unit will also be high
because each application requires a survey, and the registrar must often
inspect the land and hold special enquiries. This system was long used in
England, and met with very little success. Although the system is based on
voluntary registration, its establishment still requires a vast amount of
resources. The method is, moreover, unsuitable as a basis for a land information system.

System 2 has the same general characteristics and disadvantages as system
1, but it is expected that with system 2, it will take less time to register most of
the land. In countries where the system is in operation, it is used mainly

- in connection with land granted or sold by the Crown, which would have
  to be surveyed in any case, and where the ownership is quite clear from
  the start;

- in areas covered by good topographical maps which can be used as registration maps;

- where the boundaries follow clearly visible natural features such as
  hedges, ditches, etc., as is the case in England.

System 3 involves much lower costs per unit because all units in an area are
dealt with at the same time. The initial costs are probably higher, of course,
and will in most cases be borne mainly by the public. This can, however, be
regulated to a certain extent by restricting systematic registration to specified
.areas, and extending those areas only as fast as resources become available.

It is obvious that it is more effective to survey and register 100 units simultaneously than to pick 100 units scattered within a large district, and deal with them on separate occasions. A thorough discussion of sporadic and systematic registration can be found in works by Dowson and Sheppard (1968) and Simpson (1976). They strongly recommend systematic registration for the initial operations.

The technical aspects are also of importance in this connection. Sporadic registration seldom covers a large area at one time. Hence, the principal surveying method employed is ground surveying. When aerial photographs and photogrammetry can be used, mapping becomes considerably faster and cheaper. The costs can be kept low, however, only when a rather large area is surveyed at one time. Systematic registration makes this possible. Systematic registration also determines ownership more reliably. Announcements and enquiries are more effective, and conflicting interests of ownership, etc., are revealed automatically.

The introduction of systematic, compulsory registration within chosen areas does not, however, mean that sporadic registration cannot be used in other parts of the country. It is important that land, which must be surveyed in any case, and where ownership rights are unclouded, be registered immediately. In most of the former colonies, land sold or granted by the Crown was registered even if the plots were scattered; that is, compulsory but sporadic registration was used for this type of land.

8.7 Priorities and selection of areas

If a systematic approach is chosen, it is necessary to decide whether the long-term programme should aim at covering the total area of the country or only selected parts. In either case, it then becomes necessary to determine in which regions and districts the operations should start, and how they should continue, that is, priorities must be assigned.

It is quite possible to introduce a new or improved cadastral/land registration system in some parts of the country and not in others. There are bound to be regional differences in legislation and registration in the short term in any case. The possibility of applying the principle of selectivity and starting in areas with favourable conditions should be discussed seriously. It is advantageous for a poor country with meagre resources to be able to take one step at a time without committing itself to a project which might prove overly burdensome. Systematic cadastres/land registers are well suited to this kind of approach.

Which areas should be given highest priority? This depends, of course, on the specific problems the new or improved system is intended to solve. If the problems are mainly urban, it would be natural to start in highly urbanized areas. If the goal is to solve agricultural problems, areas with the most intensive agricultural production, the highest level of development or the most urgent problems should be considered first. In areas where farming is rather primitive, on the other hand, or where there is a lot of land available for new cultivation, one will not usually find a strong sense of property rights, or a strongly felt need for secure ownership, or a great need for investment credits. Land values will generally be low as well. In these cases, little support can be expected from the landowners.

Generally, areas with the following characteristics should be given high priority:

- Strong population pressures and competition for the land

- Great need for dwellings and difficulty in guiding the development of new settlements

- Intensive agriculture with commercial production

- High level of development or the prospect of development within previously extensive areas

- Areas with special problems such as litigation, unregulated squatting, insecure ownership, risk of fragmentation, environmental problems, etc.

However, areas with difficult conditions (with regard to land tenure, survey methods, etc.) should be avoided until the process and methods are well established.

To assign priorities to the areas, it may be appropriate to select three or four important factors and to rank each area according to these factors on a five-point scale, for example, see Fig. 8.3. This ranking could later be adjusted with regard to other relevant circumstances.

8.8 Definition of legal measures

Many people – especially those with backgrounds in surveying or other technical fields – look upon cadastre and land register as essentially technical matters. These aspects are certainly important, but fundamental is also the need for a sound legal basis for initiating as well as for operating and maintaining the system. Experience suggests that major changes in legal systems – not least those related to land – take a long time to implement. They are often emotionally charged and there may be wide differences of opinion. Consequently, the need for legal action should be considered at an early stage, and outlined in the feasibility study.

The relative importance of the legal aspects is related to the objectives of the planned system. We have already spoken about three different situations:

1. The intention is to develop a system primarily for informational purposes.

2. The intention is to develop a system primarily for fiscal purposes.

3. The intention is to develop a multipurpose system of legal land registration.

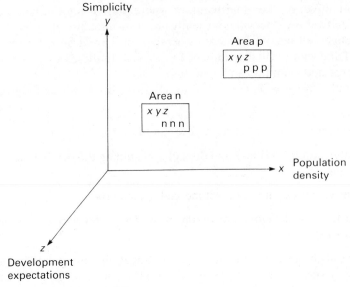

Fig. 8.3 Priority position of different areas

In the first case, the legal aspects are not particularly important. There still must be rules regarding standards and systems, data-gathering methods, obligatory provision and dissemination of information, etc. But these rules are normally of a technical or administrative nature.

The legal aspects are more important in the second case. Decrees and by-laws are needed concerning taxation and assessment, the legal status of the data in the system, the administrative structure of the organization, etc. The need for legal underpinning is greater, but even in this case, major changes in land laws or land registration ordinances are seldom needed.

If, in the third case, the main intention is to make moderate technical or administrative improvements in pre-existing cadastral/land registration systems, major legal changes may still not be necessary. But if the purpose is more far-reaching such as the introduction of a new system of title registration, it will inevitably give rise to a reassessment of the entire legal system regarding land and dealings in land. As this undoubtedly should be the main, long-term alternative in most cases, the following discussion will concentrate on this alternative.

What fundamental legal problems must then be resolved? Of course, this will differ from situation to situation and from country to country. But some general aspects will be highlighted with regard to the three following points:

● the definition of basic rights in land;

● legal powers of land registration;

● legislation concerning registration proceedings.

Definition of basic rights in land

If a legal register is to guarantee rights in land, *these rights must be clearly defined*. In many countries land rights are ambiguous and may also vary from region to region. Registration can help to clarify this situation.

This holds true for industrialized as well as for developing countries. The English system, for example, did not begin to work smoothly until the very complicated land laws were reformed in 1925. When Kenya introduced title registration even for native customary lands in the 1960s, Kenyans were also forced to ponder the nature of rights in land. Should priority be given to rights of occupancy or to full ownership; to individual rights or group rights? Customary rights were ambiguous and had changed over time. There were also regional differences. Kenya finally chose to register individual ownership whenever appropriate, which, of course, accelerated the gradual transformation from group to individual rights.

Another central issue is whether *occupancy* creates rights in land, be it public or private. This is an urgent problem in both rural and urban areas of many developing countries with rapid population growth. Often the occupant is granted a legal right to stay after having lived on the land for a certain period of time. Systematic title registration requires the resolution of the problems associated with the rights of squatters. Should they be granted ownership or occupancy rights and, in the latter case, for how long? Many planners and administrators resist the idea of giving irregular squatters the same quality of rights as more legitimate occupants. On the other hand, if a squatter settlement is to be developed and improved by self-activity, the occupants have to be given some security of tenure. The solution may be a registered limited-term lease. But this must be defined in law.

A third important question concerns the *legal status of unregistered rights*. A basic principle of title registration is that the register itself must include all information about the current status of rights, making it unnecessary to make searches outside the register. A necessary precondition is that deeds on transfers of rights in property be registered. They will otherwise be valueless against a third party in good faith, and be enforceable only as contracts between the parties involved. Rules making deed registration compulsory must, therefore, be introduced into the law.

However, it is never the case that all rights are registered. A land register normally focuses on certain major rights and encumbrances such as ownership, rights of occupancy, mortgages, some easements, charges, etc. Long-term leases may be registered while short-term ones are not. This must be resolved in the law. There may also be other rights in the property in addition to the registered rights. These may be either of a general nature, such as planning by-laws, or more specific, such as rights-of-way. The type and validity of such *overriding interests* should be defined in the law.

Legal powers of land registration

Many deed registration systems provide no other guarantees than to serve as evidence in case of double transfers or other disputes. On the other hand, strict title registration systems formally guarantee all titles inscribed, and confer the right to indemnity if a bona fide party suffers a loss because of errors in the register. In practice there may also be intermediate forms. A register of deeds can sometimes provide a high degree of security because of the old tradition of always inscribing rights, and thanks to thorough scrutiny of all deeds by the registrar. By the same token, the fact that a register is formally a register of titles is no guarantee for a high degree of legal validity. The quality of the titles is highly dependent on the extent to which all dealings in rights actually are recorded in the register.

Land registration primarily invests legal powers in the rights inscribed. If the property units are defined on maps, registration also provides evidence concerning the extent and boundaries of the property. However, this evidence seldom attains the status of a formal guarantee. Even if the boundaries are surveyed and recorded in detail, the map and the survey records will, in most countries, not be conclusive evidence of the boundary. They will be treated merely as an indication whose strength will depend on the surveying methods employed, demarcation on the ground, and whether or not there is formal approval from the parties. The law should, as far as possible, explicitly define to what extent registration will provide legal guarantees for titles as well as for boundaries.

Legislation concerning registration proceedings

A well-developed system of land registration generally includes three main steps: the surveying and demarcation of the property; the examination of title (often called adjudication, i.e. the official ascertainment of rights in land, Simpson 1976); and the registration itself. These steps, including the legislation needed, will be treated in the following chapters. Only a few remarks will be made here.

While the survey is mainly a technical matter, adjudication and registration must be carried out according to formal proceedings specified in special laws. It can be discussed whether two separate laws or a joint adjudication/registration law are preferable.

This depends largely on the particular situation. If a new land register is to be established by systematic adjudication area by area, then the work within each district can be expected to be finished at a specific time, and be carried out more or less independently of the operations of the register. A separate law will then be a natural solution. This is the alternative chosen by Kenya and Sweden for areas with unregistered property. After the initial registration is finished, the continued adjudication will be a part of the normal registration proceedings, and should then be regulated in a registration law. The same is the case if the register is compiled in a sporadic way upon application from the owner, by grant or by sale. Adjudication will then be an ongoing task linked to registration proceedings.

If adjudication is done in a systematic way and regulated in a separate law or a separate section of the law, the following components will normally be dealt with: definition of adjudication areas, officers and their duties, claims, principles of adjudication proceedings and preparation of adjudication records, complaints, appeals and irrevocability.

When the adjudication is terminated, the demarcation map and list of titles are sent to the registration office. The first registration will be completed there, and a register supported by a registration map will be established. Special rules are needed for this initial registration. But the most important part of the legal framework deals with rules about maintenance and updating. If these are not efficient and comprehensive, the land register may deteriorate in a short time.

On the whole the rules of registration have to ensure that the duties of the registrar are well defined, that he is given ample authority to examine the legality of every transaction, that registration proceedings are efficient, that the documentation is suitable and that the whole process is designed to run smoothly. Normally registration ordinances contain such elements as regulations concerning registration districts, appointment and powers of the registrar, form of register and register map, registration proceedings, effect of registration, duty to register, appeals, rectification and indemnity.

It may also be advantageous to include in the registration rules a substantive land law governing dealings in land such as purchase, inheritance, mortgage, servitudes, etc. Control measures concerning land can also be included. There may, for example, be restrictions against fragmentation and excessive subdivision, partition among heirs, exorbitant land prices, transfers to foreigners, planning restrictions, etc. A compulsory system of land registration is probably the most efficient existing means of developing public control of land transfers, land prices, land use, etc. These matters are often decided by other authorities than the land registrar, but it is the responsibility of the registrar to verify that all legal conditions for a transfer have been satisfied.

Simpson (1976) presents detailed examples of how rules concerning adjudication and registration can be formulated – especially in developing countries – against the background of British legal traditions.

There is, of course, no room in a feasibility study for detailed proposals concerning the content and form of adjudication and registration rules. But a basic discussion is needed to illuminate the complexity of introducing a new system, and to suggest which actions should be taken at an early stage to give the project a proper legal foundation.

The following chapters will entail a more detailed discussion concerning suitable proceedings for survey, adjudication and registration.

9

Cadastral surveying

Boundaries are the main object of cadastral surveying. Normally other features, such as roads, watercourses, land-use boundaries, buildings, etc., are included, but the primary purpose is to define the land unit – on the ground and in the cadastre and land register.

Cadastral surveying operations essentially include the determination of the boundaries on the ground, the survey of the boundaries, and the demarcation of the boundaries. This chapter will not treat the question of determination. We have already discussed the concepts of general and fixed boundaries. Other aspects of boundary determination will be taken up in connection with adjudication.

9.1 Surveying

To discuss in detail surveying methods for cadastral purposes would take considerably more space than the subject warrants in this study. We shall, therefore, discuss only the various technical approaches available for establishing and maintaining cadastral/land registration systems, especially in countries with scarce material and human resources.

Network of control points

In the long run all cadastral surveying should be connected to a well-developed system of control points of different orders. Even for topographical mapping, a network of primary control points is essential. Some sort of first-order triangulation is available in almost all countries. And there are usually also control points of the second, third, etc., order as well. But in the Third World it is rare that all areas experiencing development are completely covered. If all the cadastral surveys are to be connected to the system, the network must be made denser. Here, we will not discuss the traditional methods to establish a control network but refer to appropriate textbooks. In recent decades, however, new technology has developed which greatly facilitates such networks. Electro-optic measuring for large distances has long been in use. Especially in developing countries, Doppler equipment and block triangulation have proved helpful for stabilizing long triangular chains or traverses as well as for establishing new points in cases where no easy connection to conventional networks is possible. Satellite positioning is a recently developed technique. NAVSTAR GPS (the Navigation Satellite Timing And Ranging Global Positioning System) was originally planned as a navigation system for military and civil use. Signals transmitted from satellites should make almost immediate positioning possible. When all the planned satellites are in orbit, it will be relatively easy to observe a minimum of four satellites at a time. Both identification and positioning information is transmitted from each satellite. Ranges to the satellites can be determined by the modulated carrier waves of the signals from the satellites and from comparisons between the clocks in the satellites and in the receiver unit. If four satellites are observed, the three-dimensional co-ordinates and the bias between the two clocks can be calculated. Greater relative accuracy can be obtained by making simultaneous observations from two or more stations and then comparing the relative positions of the satellites (Fig. 9.1).

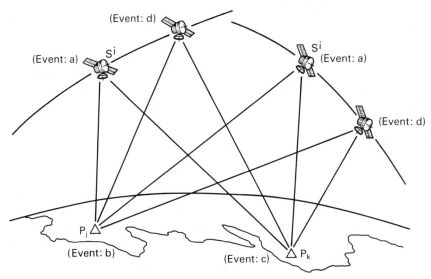

Fig. 9.1 GPS relative positioning (Wild Heerbrugg)

During the 1990s the NAVSTAR system will be fully operational, and additional similar systems are planned. Capable of determining positions within a few centimetres or less, they are very soon likely to play an important role – especially in the densification of existing control-point networks. So far the required equipment is rather expensive, but prices seem to go down rapidly. Block triangulation, another method for the densification of existing control networks, has been used a great deal during the last decades – especially in connection with photogrammetric mapping.

But even with these new technical methods, it will take a long time before all the cadastral surveys in developing countries can be connected through countrywide networks of control points. This is certainly true in the case of sporadic surveys. It is obviously easier to link the survey to absolutely positioned control points, which have been established by ground survey, photogrammetric, or satellite methods when cadastral/land registration systems are introduced in a systematic way, area by area.

Even though it would be desirable to connect all cadastral surveys to such control nets, it must be admitted that many of the cadastres and land registers, which have been established without any absolute positioning, have nevertheless worked very well. The Australian systems are examples. As noted earlier, the normal procedure in the Australian states is to make sporadic surveys without connection to a common control-point network. This means that initially there were substantial areas not covered by registration index maps, and that the only available property maps were those shown on the title certificates. Essentially the same procedure, using the Torrens system, has been applied in the western Canadian provinces.

On the other hand, it is obvious that in time it will be seen as imperative to link every property map to a common system and to have a complete picture of all the property boundaries within large areas. Such a tendency already exists in Australia and Canada. To achieve this goal the density of the control-point network is usually increased by terrestrial or photogrammetric methods. Old existing boundaries are often integrated into this system through the use of aerial photos. In Sweden, for example, a register index map on a scale of 1:10 000 has been developed for practically the whole country with the aid of aerial photos and a countrywide network of control points. Existing maps of older properties have been adapted to this system by means of photo-interpretation and field work.

The UN Ad Hoc Group of Experts on Cadastral Surveying and Land Information Systems (1985) reached the following conclusion:

> Cadastral maps and other land information systems should always be based on a network of homogeneous control points, preferably connected to the national geodetic control. Although the primary concern is that the position of each parcel must be correct relative to its immediate surroundings, longer-term considerations indicate that it should also be correct in its absolute position in space in respect of the national co-ordinate system. Investment in time and cost in establishing a good basic geodetic network is rarely wasted.

Methods for detailed surveys

Sooner or later the goal will be to establish a cadastral map which gives a total view of all the land units within the area in question. Otherwise it will be difficult to create an efficient parcel-based LIS. Even in a continent like Australia with a well-developed system of title registration, it is considered unsatisfactory to make registration maps only for every single new unit. As mentioned before (Section 5.2) there is a strong trend to get new and former surveys integrated in a general control grid, with survey plans designed to cover not only the individual land units but also whole areas.

The first question will be to find whether it is possible to compile such plans from existing topographic maps, cadastral surveys, aerial pictures, ortho-photo maps, etc. Examples from many countries have shown that this often is possible to a high degree by transforming extant cadastral maps to a common scale, so far as possible connect them to control points but otherwise try to fit in the boundaries on topographic maps, othophoto maps or other aerial photo material, of course in combination with certain field checks. If whole groups of properties are surveyed in a common local system, the group as such can be fitted in by using instruments such as planvariographs or by ordinary manual methods. If the national and the local system can be connected, computer-aided support can be used to transform the co-ordinates and plot the map. Digitizer may be used to collect co-ordinates from old cadastral maps.

If, however, new cadastral surveys are needed, these can be made with either ground survey methods or photogrammetric methods.

The main ground survey methods have been the plane table method, the orthogonal method, and the polar method.

The *plane table method* was used extensively for cadastral surveys in several European countries during the nineteenth century (Fig. 9.2 shows a plane table from 1601).

The *orthogonal method* along with the polar method, is the classical method for numerical cadastral surveys (see Fig. 9.3). Based on perpendicu-lar offsets, it can be carried out with very simple equipment and is well adapted for surveying small areas. Until recently, it was used extensively for cadastral purposes in urbanized areas in Europe. The method can be extended to larger areas if control points are established in advance and baselines are linked to the control network.

The *polar method* – also known as 'surveying by bearing and distance' – became universally popular with the development of precise optical instru-ments for measuring distance. The method has become even more important now due to the availability of electronic distance-measuring devices and data-processing equipment. Compared with the orthogonal method, its main advantages lie, firstly, in the fact that the detailed survey can be made immediately after the traverse network is established on the ground, thus reducing the number of set-ups at each station, and, secondly, in that the shape and nature of the terrain have no significant influence on the accuracy of the survey.

The appearance of self-recording electronic tachometers and automatic plotters has further developed surveying operations in the field as well as at the office. For example, the 'total station instrument' is a device which mea-sures both angles and distances and records the data electronically. At this

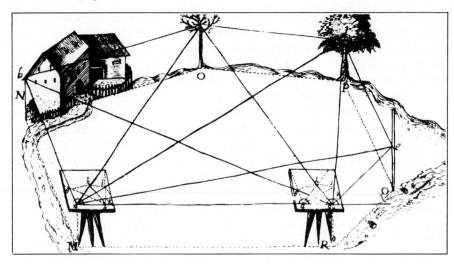

Fig. 9.2 Plane table (from Zubler 1601). It allows the map making in the open fields on the base of proportional triangles. All points are the points of intersection of the directions observed from the terminals of a base. The scale of the map results from the plotted length of the base. The maps produced were predominantly in scales of 1:1000, 1:2500, and 1:5000. A characteristic common to these surveys was that plane table positions were not monumented. Although the method results in relatively large uncertainties, experienced surveyors were able to achieve a graphical accuracy (within the range of scales mentioned) of ±20 cm to ±80 cm. Even today the plane table method can be cheap and efficient. It has the great advantage of permitting continuous comparison in the field between the actual topography and its plotted depiction.

point the data may be passed directly into a computing system for storage and processing and, where appropriate, for plotting. The devices may be used for establishing control points, especially by traversing, or for fixing points of detail, such as the turning points of property boundaries. A virtually uninterrupted flow of survey data can be provided, beginning with data acquisition in the field and ending with the desired product such as a map. The equipment is very efficient but currently much more expensive than conventional devices for measuring angles and distances.

We mentioned earlier that satellite-positioning systems such as GPS may be very efficient as well as sufficiently accurate for the determination of control points. Their usefulness for detailed cadastral survey is as yet unproven.

One use for such positioning systems is providing reference points for *photogrammetric* surveys. These may have limited application in the day-to-day recording of subdivisions, but they have great relevance for the initial establishment of a cadastre. Under favourable conditions the photogrammetric methods have many advantages over ground methods. They can be used for large areas, even when known points are widely spaced. A dense grid can then be established by photogrammetric block triangulation. The methods have a high degree of flexibility, and can be adapted to meet widely

Fig. 9.3 Orthogonal measuring in the sixteenth century. The square and the chain have long since been tools of the land surveyor. The square is a sighting device used for setting out right angles

varying requirements for accuracy, cost, and type of product. Generally, aerial photos provide more extensive information than ground methods and require less manpower for the production of cadastral maps. On the other hand, the application of photogrammetry usually requires a large investment, and the initial flying costs per unit of area will be high for small survey areas. Furthermore, aerial photos can seldom provide all the necessary information, but must be supplemented by field investigations and ground surveys. The choice of an appropriate survey method should, therefore, be based on the best combination of field and photogrammetric methods. However, in many countries legal regulations prevent, to some extent, the combination of different methods. Regulations requiring centimetre accuracy, surveying of boundary lengths, metes and bounds descriptions, etc., can effectively prevent the use of photogrammetric methods for cadastral purposes. Therefore, before the initiation of large cadastral/land registration operations, a consideration of changes in existing survey regulations may be advisable.

The many variations possible in photogrammetric methods lead to varying degrees of accuracy and expense. Cost and accuracy are influenced especially by flying height and the employment of methods which more or less eliminate the effect of topographic relief, the tilt of the camera, and other disturbing factors. The basic product is the aerial photograph itself, which can be useful for many purposes, not least for planning. However, without additional refinement it is seldom considered adequate for the documentation of property units within a large area.

We will now consider some possible methods of refinement, moving from simpler, cheaper methods to more sophisticated ones.

1. Photo-interpretation of unchecked photographs taken on an approximate scale but without correction for scale deviation. Combination of different photos to create photo-mosaics. This method was among those proposed in Ethiopia during the 1970s as a basis for cadastral mapping.

2. The enlargement of photos to a prescribed scale with the aid of some ground reference points. In the extensive work in Kenya to establish a complete land register for the country, this was the main method used in photo-interpretation and mapping.

3. Use of checked and rectified photographs. The distortions arising from differences in scale and the tilt of the camera are eliminated. This method presupposes the availability of some control points: block-triangulation or other photogrammetric methods can be used to increase the sometimes scant number. The method is widely used for cadastral or other mapping in many countries, especially in the developing countries. It can give good results in flat terrain. A transparent overlay on which the boundaries are copied produces a conventional cadastral map with an accuracy that will correspond to the drafting ability of the average draftsman.

4. A more advanced method for rectification is differential rectification, through which both tilt and height displacements are removed. For this process special orthophotographic instruments are used to convert aerial photographs from central projections to orthogonal projections. The result is an accurate photo map. However, the equipment is rather expensive and is not available in all countries. In most European countries this is the main method for photogrammetric mapping. In many cases, the orthophoto map is acceptable as it is and need not be transformed into a line map.

5. Maps produced by high-precision analogue or analytical photogrammetric instruments from photos taken (mostly) after pre-marking of the boundaries. This method is normally used as an alternative to ground surveys in European countries when substantial areas are to be surveyed at one time, for example, after reallotment or if a totally new or revised cadastral map is desired.

The marking of boundary points before beginning aerial photography is possible in all methods but is used primarily in case 5. The probability that marks will be left undisturbed varies widely and is of paramount importance in deciding whether to use such signals. To keep the costs low, cheap materials must be used – in developing countries this often means such local materials as limed tree branches, etc. Whether to pre-mark or not is determined not only by cost and the degree of accuracy desired but also by the type of land. In areas of intensive land use one can usually identify boundaries between different parcels by features such as ditches, tracks, hedges, fences, etc. In areas with extensive land use, these features are less common, and boundaries might, therefore, have to be premarked so as to make them visible and well defined in the aerial photographs.

Choice of method

As mentioned earlier, cadastral surveys should be implemented through the appropriate combination of terrestrial and photogrammetric methods. The methods chosen depend on the circumstances, and no general recommendations can be given. However, the following factors should be considered.

First, it must be decided if *existing* aerial photographs of the area in question are sufficient for cadastral purposes. In a 1987 report Lundgren states:

> Experiences from a project in Zambia revealed the weakness of using old aerial photographs for this kind of mapping. Fields, footpaths, roads, etc., tend to change their location over time, a phenomenon confirmed in the project where 10-year-old aerial photographs were used. Generally, one can assume that the more developed the agricultural practices are in the area, the more stable is the structure of the properties. In Kenya, where enlarged aerial photographs are used for cadastral mapping purposes they normally don't use photographs which are older than five years. Quite natural, the best results of mapping are achieved when recent aerial photographs are available. Normally, the aerial photography necessary for the cadastral mapping programme should form a part of the National aerial photography programme. The possibilities of multipurpose use of the photographs will reduce the costs for the particular cadastral application.

Whether or not older aerial photographs should be used depends also on the negative scale. For the production of cadastral register maps, enlargement as great as six or eight times seems to give acceptable results.

If *new* aerial photography is needed, it will as a rule be economically feasible to use photogrammetric methods only when fairly large areas can be covered at the same time. If the cadastral survey is made systematically, area by area, this is usually possible, while ground methods must generally be used in sporadic surveys such as in the day-to-day recording of subdivisions.

The choice of methods also depends on the nature of the area, especially its topography, vegetation, and boundary system. In a hilly area the photogrammetric methods (1–3) described above may result in unacceptable errors, in which case more expensive methods must be used. With a heavy cover of vegetation only parts of the boundaries are visible, and, if photogrammetric methods are used at all, it may be necessary to supplement the aerial photography with rather extensive ground surveying. When only a few boundaries are physically demarcated or visible in the photographs, premarking or ground surveying must be used. Generally, the use of aerial photos is most advantageous in open country with small, irregular fields having visible limits. Ground surveying here will be expensive because of the irregular boundaries.

Whether aerial survey is competitive with ground surveying also depends on the wage scale and other available resources. If the wages are low and if the technical resources for photogrammetric surveys are meagre, ground surveying has a competitive edge. When designing a system for cadastral surveys, one has to remember that aerial mapping is bound to come into play more and more for the initial registration, especially when one of the cheaper methods (1–4) is considered adequate. It is, therefore, advisable for the planned system to include aerial mapping, starting with the most likely areas. Generally speaking, this means areas large enough for economical map production and with clearly visible property boundaries.

Considering the degree of accuracy required, it must be admitted that most of the benefits of cadastre/land-registration systems can be achieved even with rather low mapping standards. Even simple maps, like the Swedish economic map on a scale of 1:10 000, have proved adequate in rural areas for the unique identification of all properties and as the basis for a register of title with a guarantee of ownership and other mandated rights (see Fig. 9.4). This has also been true in Kenya, where the title register is based mainly on the photo-interpretation of enlarged – often unrectified – aerial photos on a scale of 1:2500, which give indefeasible titles with 'general boundaries'. These titles are almost always accepted for sales, mortgages, taxation, planning, public administration, etc. Even simple large-scale maps make possible the identification of the plot on the ground and thus secure the connection to the land.

This is not to say that additional advantages could not be gained by switching to more precise methods. If the boundary demarcations should be lost or if there is litigation concerning them, a good map will be valuable as evidence. But it will not be decisive unless the boundaries were fixed at the survey in the presence of all parties. It is also evident that highly accurate maps are useful for many other purposes. In the industrialized countries there is a definite trend towards the establishment of digitized multipurpose base maps of high standard, at least in urban areas.

But to emphasize the claim made earlier, the most important advantages of cadastres/land registration can be achieved with rather simple maps. Therefore Dale (1983) argues that graphic standards of accuracy for the recording and plotting of boundaries meet the necessary requirements for good land administration, but that excessive precision tends to have a detrimental effect, creating dispute and conflict where none previously existed.

As an example of cadastral surveying methods in practice, we can examine the programme chosen in Thailand for land outside the urban centres (see Williamson 1983):

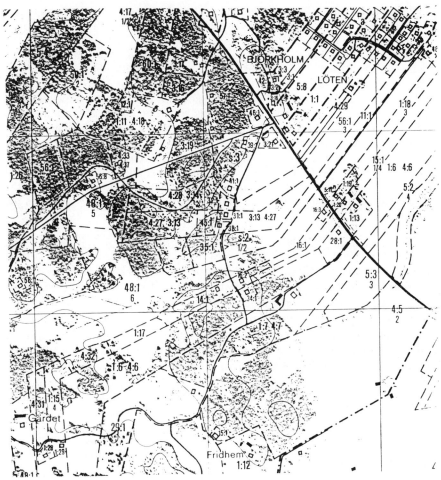

Fig. 9.4 Swedish economic map, produced from orthophoto and including all boundaries

Approximately 80% are based on rectified photomaps at 1:4000 in rural areas and 20% on traverse and tape surveys at 1:1000 in village and urban areas. The survey process based on rectified photomaps is as follows:

a) photography was flown at 2300 m with a wide-angle camera, resulting in a photoscale of 1:15000. The photography was flown with 2 km between flight lines with 80% end lap and 42% side lap. No signalisation of boundaries or other control points was carried out in the field;

b) four horizontal control points are determined by ground methods from the cadastral control. Occasionally photogrammetric control is determined by the Department using aerotriangulation techniques; the Department has the equipment and access to a recent 'model' block adjustment programme for this purpose. Vertical control for the adjustment is scaled off the existing topographic mapping since the rectified photomaps obviously show no heights or contours;

c) rectified photomaps are prepared at 1:4000 on a 500 mm × 500 mm format, representing 2 km × 2 km on the ground. It should be noted that virtually all legally developed land in Thailand is relatively flat and is consequently ideally suited to the use of rectified photomaps, and

d) the photomaps are used only for issuing land titles in those areas where the physical boundaries of each parcel are clearly visible on the photograph. In such case the adjudication process and marking of corners are as described previously. Boundaries are measured but angles are not measured. In the presence of all adjoining owners, the boundaries are marked on the photomap and on a transparent overlay. Corners and corner numbers are also marked on the photomap. Areas are determined graphically.

In locations where the boundaries are not visible from the photomap, the surveys are carried out based on the co-ordinated traverses, but only tapes and optical squares are used; sometimes the triangle survey method is adopted and only the tape is used. The cadastral map is plotted at 1:1000 to 1:4000, depending on the detail.

In conclusion, for initial cadastral/land registration work covering large areas, photogrammetric methods should be used in combination with corresponding ground surveys. If survey personnel, technical equipment, and technical know-how are in short supply, simple mapping methods must be chosen, as a rule using enlarged or rectified aerial photographs in flat areas; orthophotos, if possible, in hilly areas. If the boundaries are not clearly visible, simple signalization may be considered. In developing countries maps produced by high-precision photogrammetric instruments are probably economically feasible only for some urbanized areas or if the map is produced primarily for purposes other than cadastres/land registration. Resources are simply too meagre and the necessary work too extensive to permit the use of expensive methods.

9.2 Demarcation

Demarcation is an operation which includes both legal and technical aspects. Let us consider two types of case.

1. The exact position of the boundaries is fixed on the ground in the presence of the parties. If a dispute arises, the boundary is determined by an officer or a court with the right of appeal. After the positions of the boundaries have been fixed, they are permanently marked with pipes, stones, concrete beacons, etc., if existing fences, hedges, and ditches are not considered sufficient demarcation.

2. The boundaries are, as far as possible, recognized on the ground. When necessary, they may be surveyed or identified in aerial photos in combination with simple ground surveying, but they are neither legally fixed nor permanently demarcated if this is not requested by the parties.

The first method is usually, but not necessarily, combined with accurate ground surveys or large-scale aerial surveys with pre-marking. In principle it is important to differentiate between the concept of legally fixed boundaries and the concept of an accurate survey. If the boundary is determined in the presence of the parties and then protected by good permanent beacons, or if it can be re-created on the basis of permanent control points or from good aerial photos, then it is evident that simple and inexpensive survey methods can be used.

Method 1 is the normal one where new boundaries are being established, as in subdivisions, Crown grants, property consolidation, etc., if the parties do not choose to rely on semi-permanent features such as fences, hedges, walls, etc., instead of beacons. This method is also normally used for sporadic registration within an existing layout, when good large-scale maps such as the English Ordnance map are not available.

It is, however, obvious that the second method is much cheaper in most of those cases where a register map for a large area is being established for the first time, especially where the boundaries are visible on aerial photos. Even then, field work must always play a part in the determination of the correct boundaries. But it is quite another matter to make detailed determinations of all boundaries on the ground, and then to fix their positions with permanent marks. Experience also shows that the parties may often agree on the general position of a boundary but disagree on its precise location. Method 1, therefore, may lead to lengthy disputes or even litigation.

So even if method 1 does provide greater certainty for the future, it is very doubtful whether a developing country has the necessary resources. This is especially true when there are few existing surveys of ownership in customary land so that the work must be started from scratch. Then, it is probably wiser to use simple methods so as to gain the big advantage of registration as soon as possible. Boundaries can be fixed and demarcated wholly or partially at a later date, if and when the authorities or parties find this to be so essential as to justify the high costs.

It may be appropriate to note some reservations about these general recommendations. In areas where few physical boundaries exist so that a detailed discussion in the presence of the parties is necessary in any case, demarcation would be quite valuable, and would not add much to the total workload. Another relevant factor is whether the system of boundaries is closely spaced and irregular (as is often the case in areas with terraced fields) or sparse and regular.

The discussion above has focused on only two main types of demarcation systems. In practice many kinds of intermediate types may be found. Thus it is common in several countries for boundaries to be determined in the presence of the parties but seldom permanently demarcated. Instead, physical features such as low ridges, footpaths, field and crop limits, etc., are accepted as sufficient demarcation. In cases where no visible boundaries exist, stones, etc., may be erected, or the parties may simply be advised to put up fences or hedges themselves. In Kenya, for example, temporary demarcation has been a normal procedure and the authorities have tried – though not always with success – to get the boundaries planted with hedges.

In general, the type of procedure and the existing boundary system are of great importance in deciding on the system of demarcation. Other important factors are the resources available, the urgency of the programme, and the extent to which most boundaries are visible on the ground. Instead of such relevant factors, however, a desire for technical perfection often seems to have determined the methods of both surveying and demarcation, and economic factors have seldom been given due consideration.

10

Adjudication

10.1 The legal role of adjudication

Lawrance (1985) describes the concept of adjudication in the following way:

> Adjudication is the word now used in many English-speaking countries to describe the process whereby all existing rights in a particular parcel of land are finally and authoritatively ascertained. The equivalent word in French-speaking countries is 'constatation'. This specialized use of the word 'adjudication' is of recent origin. It was first introduced in the 1950s to replace 'settlement', the word previously used to describe systematic ascertainment of rights in land; use of the word 'settlement' was causing confusion, for it is usually taken to mean settlement of persons on land, a process sometimes referred to as 'colonization'.

Adjudication is, according to Lawrance, an essential prerequisite for certain other land measures:

- Land registration (registration of title)
- Land consolidation
- Disposition of state land.

As discussed in Chapter 8, adjudication is a necessary measure in case of registration of titles. When a parcel is first entered into the register, particulars of all rights and liabilities in it must have been ascertained and determined conclusively. This must also be the case when consolidation is undertaken, if a satisfactory record of parcels and rights in land does not already exist, as the entitlement to a consolidated holding is determined on the basis of the classified land values of all parties. Adjudication is a prerequisite for disposition of state land, too. Without adjudication the boundaries between state land and private land might often be vague. There may even be holdings, occupancy rights or customary rights on portions of the 'unoccupied' land. In some countries adjudication of state land has been a major task.

In Sri Lanka for example, 'settlement' was the main work of the Survey Department for several decades. In northern Sweden where rights to large tracts of forested land had earlier been uncertain, demarcation of state land from village lands or other private holdings was an important measure during the eighteenth and nineteenth centuries. This was not solely a question of objective boundary determination. The interests in, and rights to, land were vague. Because of this, public policy could play a major role. Depending on the prevailing policy, the principles of demarcation were influenced by aspects
of taxation, colonization and/or the requirements of the iron or forest industries.

Land tenure policy may also influence the principles of adjudication as a prerequisite for the registration of titles. Indeed, according to Simpson (1976, p. 195)

> it is a cardinal principle of adjudication that it does not, by itself, alter existing rights or create new ones. It merely establishes with certainty and finality what rights exist, by whom they are exercised, and to what limitation, if any, they are subject.

The situation is however often complex, especially in areas where customary rules prevail.

> Registration of some of the existing customary rights ascertained by adjudication may be regarded as undesirable on ground of policy. It will almost invariably be necessary to convert an ascertained customary right to what is considered to be its equivalent under registration or conveyancing legislation. An example of adjudication as an instrument of land policy is provided by Kenya, where in the 1950s it was government policy to convert customary tenure to full individual ownership in order to promote agricultural development. Persons found on adjudication to possess a customary right to occupy and use land were to be adjudged as *owners* of that land and their title was to be absolute; any limitation exercised by tribal authorities on this occupation and use of customary land were to disappear. No provision was made for registration of land held by groups, such as a clan; if group ownership was revealed by adjudication, the land had to be divided into individual holdings.(Provision for adjudication and registration of group land has since been made.)

The problem of individual or group registration is discussed in another part of this study. It suffices to state here that even if adjudication formally is only the definition and recording of existing rights, it may still be influenced by the prevailing land policy and play a decisive role for the development of these rights.

10.2 Different forms of adjudication

Theoretically the structural forms of adjudication can be classified in many ways.The division between *sporadic* and *systematic* adjudication has, however, a decisive influence on the whole proceeding and will be chosen as the main basis of classification.

It is obvious from the earlier discussion that there are many advantages to systematic registration, and thus also to systematic adjudication, from the point of view of cost efficiency as well as multipurpose use. In reality, however, sporadic adjudication is still the most common in the Third World. Sporadic adjudication may be voluntary or compulsory. If voluntary, it is as a rule initiated by the owner or occupier, and this is usually the case even when sporadic registration is compulsory. However, when the process is compulsory, the land registrar is often empowered to adjudicate and register at his own discretion without waiting for an application. Normally the costs of sporadic adjudication and registration are wholly or partly borne by the applicant. Adjudication is mainly needed as a prerequisite for registration when registration is supposed to guarantee the rights, extent and boundaries of the property, that is, when a land unit is registered for the first time in a system of title registration or a well-developed system of deeds registration. If the unit is not established as a state grant or by subdivision of a registered property, the titles and valid rights in the unit must be tested by investigation of earlier transfers or by special proceedings.

Irrespective of whether they are voluntary or compulsory, the proceedings may be of a *judicial* or *administrative* nature. In the first case the disputes are handled by an ordinary court or a special land tribunal, and in the second case by the registrar, specially appointed adjudication authorities or other administrative officers. However, even in an administrative process, it is as a rule possible to appeal finally to an established court such as the High Court. Judicial proceedings have been the norm in French-speaking countries, while an administrative process is used in many English-speaking countries.

Generally, judicial proceedings may provide more proper legal treatment in the first instance. But on the other hand, they tend to cause lengthy and costly proceedings. Legal assistance is often considered necessary, but the costs are not always affordable. In cases where the disputing parties have very different economic situations, a formal judicial process may, therefore, sometimes produce less equitable results than an administrative one. From many practical viewpoints it may be an advantage to keep the initial adjudication stages administrative rather than judicial.

This is still more important when adjudication is systematic. If the goal is to cover an entire area, the adjudication must, of course, be compulsory, meaning that, in most cases, the bulk of the costs must be defrayed by the public. Since an adjudication with many properties and individuals involved is always a delicate matter, simple and less costly proceedings should be chosen in which elements of negotiation play a major role. Systematic adjudication is, therefore, almost always based on an administrative proceeding, including determination of disputes in the first instance.

In most countries well-developed routines for sporadic adjudication and registration already exist. We will not describe them further. As this study focuses on methods to establish and maintain or improve systems of cadastre/

land registration, not least in developing countries, the systematic approach deserves the greatest attention. In the following we will, therefore, discuss some of the main features in the process of systematic adjudication.

10.3 Adjudication by conversion of existing registers

When it comes time to introduce the reform in a country, other land-recording systems may already be in operation. Lawrance (1985) describes the situation in the following way:

> If the pre-existing record consists of a land register, the new register can be compiled merely by transcribing the particulars contained in the old register. This is a simple clerical process and adjudication is not involved. In most countries, however, the pre-existing records will consist of a register of deeds. If the deeds register is efficiently operated, it will enable a form of adjudication, often referred to as 'deeds conversion' or 'conversion of deeds register', to be adopted. This involves a systematic examination of the registered deeds, carried out in the registry office by the land registrar or other officer appointed for the purpose. Persons possessing land rights are not required to submit applications or to attend before the land registrar; a notice of intention to register is served on them, giving them the opportunity to object within a stipulated time. The land registrar then determines objections, if any, and first registration is effected. This form of adjudication is obviously quicker and less expensive than the formal systematic adjudication, carried out in the field, which is the alternative form.

Simpson (1976 pp. 208–12) gives some examples of different methods used for conversion of a deeds register: from Singapore, Penang, Malacca, Zambia and Kenya. Land registers were also compiled by conversion of deeds registers with 'appropriate opportunity for challenge and judicial investigations' in a number of European countries. Best known is the conversion in Germany at the end of the nineteenth century. A gradual conversion has also taken place in Sweden by indexing all properties, registering their rights on separate folios and providing progressively increased guarantees for all registered rights.

Conversion may often be undertaken as a gradual process, where different steps are taken to improve existing land registers or fiscal records. Figure 10.1 gives examples of such steps. It is important to make registration compulsory, to standarize and simplify the transfer and registration process and, at the same time, to provide for a more thorough examination of deeds and parties. If the registered land units are given unique identification numbers, all transactions can be noted on a separate folio for each unit, which will help prepare for the transaction to a title register. Register index map-sheets can be produced from existing map material, possibly with the aid of aerial photo interpretation and some field checks. Automation may or may not be introduced at this stage, but it can be very helpful for cross-checking existing land registers and revenue records, and would certainly facilitate the entire upgrading operation. After further checks of existing registers and records, the time might be ripe for conversion to an efficient title registration system, perhaps preceded by provisional registers, which automatically become permanent after a prescribed period.

The choice between adjudication by conversion of existing registers or adjudication in the field is not an either/or question. Even when adjudication is primarily implemented by official, systematic examination of existing registers in the office with the opportunity to object at a later date, some field work is normally needed. When, on the other hand, the work is mainly done in the field, documentary evidence and existing registers may be of assistance.

A general rule is that conversion of older registers to registers of title can only be accomplished without considerable field work when the bulk of the referred land units have already been defined on maps, and the existing registers have a comparatively high legal validity. This is especially true when the registrar routinely examines all deeds before registration to ensure their consistency with deeds already registered. Another good basis is, of course, a reliable and complete cadastre. If the existing registers are only 'passive' deeds registers without complete coverage, it is seldom worth the time to try to convert them mainly by clerical means. The natural solution would then be systematic adjudication in the field combined with the opportunity to present claims and objections and make appeals later on. In the following the main features of such a proceeding are presented in a rather normative way. Variations are naturally possible, but, in practice, the methods described have been proved to work in many cases.

10.4 The process of systematic adjudication

Priorities

Let us assume that the delicate task of establishing a legal basis for systematic adjudication and registration is finished. Whether the adjudication ordinance should be separate or not has been discussed earlier. Let us further assume that the government has determined the areas to be given priority. For many reasons, it is advisable to start in just one or two districts. In a country with no previous experience of this type of operation, there is bound to be a lack of relevant knowledge. Experience and training must develop successively. There is often a shortage of material resources as well: money, aircraft for photogrammetric mapping, offices for registration, etc. Later on adjudication and registration may be carried out in different regions of the country concurrently.

We have spoken earlier about some factors which may determine the order of priority. In the initial phase, areas should be chosen which are rather easy to survey and which are free from overly-complex patterns of land tenure. The government then officially declares the selected areas to be adjudication areas where the new legislation applies, and where compulsory, systematic adjudication can start immediately.

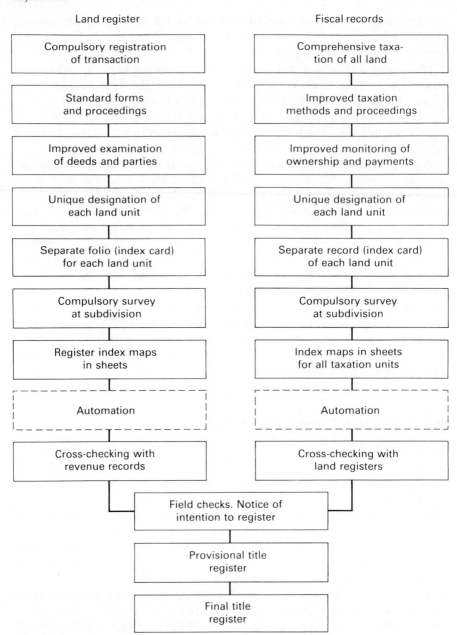

Land register	Fiscal records
Compulsory registration of transaction	Comprehensive taxation of all land
Standard forms and proceedings	Improved taxation methods and proceedings
Improved examination of deeds and parties	Improved monitoring of ownership and payments
Unique designation of each land unit	Unique designation of each land unit
Separate folio (index card) for each land unit	Separate record (index card) of each land unit
Compulsory survey at subdivision	Compulsory survey at subdivision
Register index maps in sheets	Index maps in sheets for all taxation units
Automation	Automation
Cross-checking with revenue records	Cross-checking with land registers

Field checks. Notice of intention to register

Provisional title register

Final title register

Fig. 10.1 Steps for improvement and conversion of land records

Adjudication staff

If, as is recommended, the process is to be administrative in nature, an organization or person must be appointed to lead the operations. Sometimes this task is assigned to the registrar. However, since registrars normally do not have field organizations, this is hardly to be recommended. It would appear preferable to establish a special staff for the area in question, headed by an adjudication officer who is appointed by the government. His functions are described in the following way by Lawrance (1985):

> His duties are basically administrative, although he exercises judicial functions in determining disputes and must obviously be conversant with the law, customary or statute, pertaining in the area. The adjudication process has also been described as an 'exercise in public relations'. The qualities required in an adjudication officer should match all these needs. Among his duties are:
>
> (i) The division of the declared adjudication area into smaller units known as 'adjudication sections'.
>
> (ii) The publication of all notices required by law.
>
> (iii) Explanations to the public in the adjudication area of the procedures involved.
>
> (iv) Safeguarding the interests of government in the adjudication area.
>
> (v) Determination of initial disputes referred to him by demarcation or recording officers and of subsequent final objections to the adjudication record.
>
> In carrying out these duties he is specifically empowered to issue directions to the demarcation, recording and survey officers and may himself perform demarcation and recording functions.

The officers mentioned above are part of the adjudication staff. It is a matter of convenience whether all these types of officers should be appointed. They represent different types of functions which must be carried out. But two or three functions can sometimes be executed by one person.

The demarcation officer determines existing boundaries together with the parties involved and ensures that the boundaries are indicated on the ground in a manner suitable for surveying. He should be given the power to straighten or in other ways adjust boundaries with the consent of owners, and also to make reservations for roads or paths needed. The survey officer will be responsible for the demarcation map, while the recording officer has the duty of recording claims and entering any non-disputed claims that he considers valid.

Often the official staff is supported by committees chosen among the land-owners concerned. With their local knowledge, such committees can be extremely helpful when recording and determining interests in land. They can also serve as links between the working officers and the owners or cultivators for relaying information, straightening out misunderstandings and stimulating co-operation. Sometimes – as in Kenya – the committee not only gives advice but also decides on adjudication matters and takes active part in solving disputes concerning rights to land. Lawrance comments on this as follows:

> On the face of it, active participation by committees of non-officials in the actual execution of the adjudication process is an attractive idea, particularly where the land to be adjudicated is held under customary law. It can help to inspire the trust and confidence of the public in the process. Committees of local people, particularly tribal 'elders', will always possess a better understanding of local customs relating to land than adjudication staff, many of whom may be recruited from other

parts of the country. Participation by committees of local people in the adjudication process can be at three levels. First, 'full participation' where committees are made entirely responsible for all decisions involved in various important parts of the process, including ascertainment of existing rights and determination of disputes. Second, 'partial participation' where committees are actively involved in one part of the process only and are not necessarily empowered to make the final decisions. Third, 'advisory participation' where committees are restricted to giving advice to the adjudication authority. So far as 'full participation' is concerned, committees cannot of course operate without the support of government staff, who keep the necessary records, act as 'executive officers' of committees determining disputes, ensure effective demarcation of parcels and carry out the necessary survey and mapping requirements. It is, however, the committees which make the decisions.

Publicity

In countries such as Kenya where adjudication has been successful, much attention has been paid to publicity through local newspapers, local radio, notices in public places, etc., before the work starts. It is, of course, of utmost importance that all parties involved be aware of what is going on so that they may put forward their claims. After the adjudication is finished in an area, rights in land will legally be null and void if not recorded – at least if registration has final, rather than only provisional, status. Extensive publicity is, therefore, needed. The publicity also aims at informing all persons concerned of the purpose, benefits and methods of the process as well as about the part they will have to play. The publicity should also include a notice requiring submission of claims to rights within a specified period, if the claims are not made in the field.

After the public information channels have been used, a general information meeting is arranged with the participation of the authorities, officers and interested parties. The property owners are often slightly suspicious, perhaps fearing that the process is mainly being used for taxation purposes. As full co-operation is essential, ample time should be made available for information about the use and importance of land registration.

Adjudication sections, investigation of documentary evidence

Before the actual work is started, the area should be divided into a number of adjudication sections, and documentary evidence concerning rights in land within the area in question should be collected. Lawrance (1985) presents the following viewpoints concerning the division into sections:

> The section is the basic unit of adjudication; parcels are numbered consecutively and the adjudication record is compiled section by section. On registration the adjudication section is adopted as the registration section, the basic unit of the land

register. It is referred to by the same name as that accorded to the adjudication section and retains the same numbering of parcels. Adjudication sections should, as far as possible, coincide with recognized territorial divisions (e.g. a parish or a subdivision of an administrative district) and its 'distinctive name', accorded by the adjudication officer, should be familiar to the local population. Various considerations are likely to determine the size of the sections to be declared. One such consideration is the number of parcels in the section. For convenient operation of the land registry it is useful to avoid, if possible, creating sections with an exceptionally large or an exceptionally small total of parcels. In very broad terms a total between 100 and 600 is a convenient figure.

Before the start of the field operations, relevant documentary evidence should be collected concerning rights in land within the section in question. Where reliable records exist, their information should, of course, be used. In areas with customary land rights, however, such written information is often totally lacking. In other areas an old registration system may often exist, but usually so incomplete or possessing such low legal status that complicated searches just do not pay. In such cases it may be better to collect only easily available written information while otherwise relying mainly on the claims and the field work.

When, for example, Sweden wanted to speed up the adjudication work in some problem areas of the country during the 1960s, it relieved the adjudication officer of the responsibility of making his own thorough investigations of documentary evidence, instead stressing the responsibility of the parties to submit their claims. This worked very well, as evidenced by a great increase in the amount of land processed at the same time as very few registration mistakes were reported.

Before starting the field operations, the adjudication officer publishes a note of adjudication applying to the first adjudication section in the area. The notice requires any person claiming rights in land within the described section to submit a claim in writing or in person within a stipulated period. Claims can also be made verbally at the time of recording, especially in the case of customary land.

Preparation of a demarcation map

Survey methods have been discussed in a previous chapter. The determination of boundaries is, however, not a purely technical problem; it has legal and practical implications as well. Normally this phase entails notification of the interested parties in advance, requesting that they be present in the field on a specified day. The demarcation officer (usually a surveyor) then inspects the boundaries and makes a note of any dispute.

There is often a shortage of qualified surveyors. Considerable savings in time are possible if the owners and cultivators co-operate and pre-mark their boundaries in a simple way before the official demarcation starts. This might be organized by the elected committee, possibly with help of a demarcation assistant of lower rank.

After demarcation the boundaries are surveyed – terrestrially, by photo-interpretation or in other ways discussed in Chapter 9 – and a demarcation map is prepared. The surveyor will usually make note of claims of owner-ships, occupancies and other interests as well as disputes. In this case, how-ever, lengthy discussions about rights and examination of deeds should not be combined with surveying in the field. Such is better conducted in a temporary office in the neighbourhood. Alternatively, the investigation and recording of claims can be carried out by a special recording officer. In case of disputes he will try to reach an agreement between the claimants; if this fails the dispute must be settled by the adjudication officer or by the officer and the elected committee together.

When the field work and the enquiries have been completed, the surveyor prepares a demarcation map and a preliminary list of rights to the land units, noting which boundaries and claims are still disputed. The list is often known as an adjudication record. It should, in principle, contain all the information which will be shown in the land register.

Examination of claims, final adjudication and appeals

The further examination of claims and boundaries is normally done by the adjudication officer in co-operation with the elected committee. The adjudi-cation record and the demarcation map are checked against local knowledge, and the disputes are investigated in the presence of the parties involved. As a rule most disputes are solved in this way. The demarcation map and the records are thereafter made available for inspection in a public place in the locality or in the local adjudication office. A fixed time (for example a month) is set aside for objections. Adequate publicity must be given to ensure that all parties involved – including absentees – have the opportunity to object before adjudication is completed. Objections are formally settled by the adjudi-cation officer, after hearing the committee or in co-operation with it. The adjudication officer then makes a record of the proceedings and issues a certificate of finality, which marks the end of adjudication in the section.

All countries grant the right to appeal decisions reached in the local pro-ceedings. The appeal can be made to the regional or central government or to a higher court. It is advisable to limit the right of appeal to one instance. Lengthy court proceedings must be avoided if systematic adjudication is to proceed in a satisfactory way. It cannot be stressed too strongly that an extensive appeals system with a large amount of legal processing will impede and sometimes stop the work of systematic title registration. The process must contain a substantial element of sound, practical management with ample opportunity for resolving disputes and making decisions in the field. It is probably preferable to have simple procedures leading only to presumptive title, which will automatically become absolute after some prescribed period, than to have a complicated adjudication process leading directly to absolute titles.

When the revised demarcation map and the adjudication records are declared final by the adjudication officer, they are sent to the registration office for first registration. If appeals are made, this should not stop registration, but a note is inserted in the register stating that the title in question is pending.

11

Registration

The goal of adjudication is to establish a land register with a great degree of legal validity. This would seem to be self-evident, but is not so. In some countries – such as Nepal, India and several others – careful cadastral surveys are carried out which include extensive adjudication work. But the final result is a land record, designed primarily to serve revenue purposes, and not making possible the registration of rights such as mortgages, etc. This is quite understandable from a historical point of view, but none the less such records only offer a few of the advantages of a complete and reliable register of titles. Sometimes a systematic adjudication is followed by a voluntary registration, which means that the register itself only includes a portion of the lots. This, of course, reduces considerably the value of the register.

It must be stressed that the results of adjudication – including not only ownership but also other interests in the land – automatically and as soon as possible be transferred to a land register. If adjudication is systematic, the final goal should be a register of titles. This type of register will be discussed in more detail below. Some viewpoints will then be given concerning registration procedures, especially the problem of keeping a register up to date, that is, of maintaining it. The question of automation of a register will be treated in Chapter 13.

11.1 The content of the register

The survey documentation and maps have been dealt with earlier, here concentration will be on the records.

Some technical descriptions of the property are needed even in a legal land register. The property unit must be uniquely identified, and various systems are used. In most parts of the USA, for example, the land is divided into quadrants one mile by one mile which are named after their geographical location. Normally the quadrants are further subdivided into the NW, NE, SW and SE quadrants. The next subdivision may be described as NW1/4SW1/4, that is, the northwest quarter of the southwest quarter and so on. In some other countries an identification by co-ordinates is proposed. The most usual system, however, is to number the parcels. The numbers should be simple and easy to locate. Therefore, they should refer to administrative units, normally subdivided into natural sections. Such sections may, in rural areas, consist of villages or parts of villages; in towns they consist of wards, street blocks or other natural units. These sections may be referred to by names or by numbers. It is an advantage if the section size is so small that the original parcel number will be less than 1000. These questions are further discussed in Appendix A.

Successively, however, the number of parcels will increase because of subdivision. In this case both parts or only the new parcel may be given the nearest available number. The method causes some disturbances in the regular numbering, and may make it difficult to locate the parcel on the map. Other methods are sub-numbers or sub-letters. This makes it easy to find new parcels on the map as the original order is not disturbed. It may, of course, lead to rather complicated combinations in case of excessive subdivision.

The registration map is also part of the unique identification system. Sometimes – as in the Australian states – this map is drafted on the certificate of ownership, the original of which is kept in the registry, with a copy being given to the owner. More often it is shown on map-sheets or as both a map for the single parcel and a total map for the whole section or for a map area covered by a standard-size sheet. Scales between 1:2 500 and 1:5 000 are common for rural areas, while larger scales are used in urban or well-populated areas. Even if the survey is photogrammetric, line maps are normally used. However, orthophoto maps may also be considered as registration maps.

If an official system of cadastre or property records exists in the country, the registration map is part of this system. The cadastre also gives the main description of the property. It may be restricted to the parcel number, its location, area and a reference number of the original grant or subdivision or some other way of establishing the unit. But it may also contain more information such as the amount of arable land, land classes, land value or taxation value, buildings, etc. Further details may be provided in the same record or in connected records about planning regulations, the state of the buildings, co-ordinates or centroid points of the parcel, environmental information, certain rights connected to the property such as rights of way, other servitudes, common property and so on. The unique identification makes it possible to combine all sorts of property information in a common system, and successively to expand it. The system will then often consist of a central record containing a few essential particulars about the unit and a system of connected records with further information.

If such a separate descriptive system of the land units exists, the legal land register should not duplicate the property descriptions, but should merely provide the unique property number and establish a separate folio for each land unit. When, however, there is no cadastre or official land record system, a certain amount of property description is normally provided in the legal land register itself. It then contains a *property section* with the name of the administrative unit, block name or number, parcel number, area, ways of establishing the unit, appurtenances connected to the land, etc.

A land register of the title type also contains a *proprietorship section* with the name and (often) the address of the proprietor, the reference number of the deed giving him the title, often the date of the deed and purchase price if any, and often notes of any inhibitions, cautions or restrictions affecting the right to disposition. Normally, the special encumbrances attached to a property are recorded separately in an *encumbrances section*, containing statements of mortgages, charges, leases, etc.

The delimitation of each section is not quite fixed. In some countries, rights of ownership and rights of occupancy or long-term leases are shown in separate registers, sometimes on separate folios but in the same register, and sometimes on the same folio but in different sections. Thus, in many European countries, leases are presented in the encumbrances section. Servitudes may be shown in the property section or in the encumbrances section, depending partly on how strongly they are affixed to the property. If a servitude depends on an agreement between two parties and is given priority according to the date of registration, the best place to record it seems to be in the encumbrances section. If, on the other hand, the servitude is valid against all parties, independent of any priority scheme and thus a fixed part of the property itself, it may better be displayed in the property section. Servitudes and old rights connected to the property may also be valid without any registration, and can then be treated as overriding interests. In that case, the types of interests having this overriding character ought to be stated in laws and regulations.

11.2 Form of the register

So much for the content of the register. The form as such may vary. It is not self-evident that the register should be a written one. If advanced data processing is used, the register may be replaced by a data bank. A system of this type is now used in Sweden. The question of data processing will be discussed later.

If, however, a manual register is to be kept, it ought to have a folio or card for each land unit. In cases of fragmentation where each owner has many parcel numbers, having so many folios may be impractical, especially when all mortgages and other rights are common for the entire holding. In European systems, a common folio, showing the numbers of all included parcels, is often assigned to the total holding.

If folios are used, they should not be bound together but kept in loose-leaf

Amtsgericht München
Grundbuch von Neuried   **Band** 3 **Blatt** 45   **Bestandsverzeichnis** Einlegebogen 1

Lfd. Nr. der Grundstücke	Bisherige lfd.Nr.d. Grundstücke	Bezeichnung der Grundstücke und der mit dem Eigentum verbundenen Rechte		Größe		
		Gemarkung Flurstück	Wirtschaftsart und Lage	ha	a	qm
		a / b	c			
1	2	3		4		
1	–	Neuried 116/2	Eichenweg 3, Wohnhaus, Werkstätte, Hofraum, Hf (900 qm), Garten (1500 qm)	--	24	00
2	–	Neuried 116/3	Eichenweg 5, Hf (1050 qm), Garten (1400 qm)	--	24	50

Amtsgericht München
Grundbuch von Neuried   **Band** 3 **Blatt** 45   **Erste Abteilung** Einlegebogen 1

Lfd. Nr. der Eintragungen	Eigentümer	Lfd. Nr. der Grundstücke im Bestandsverzeichnis	Grundlage der Eintragung
1	2	3	4
1	K l e i n Georg, Landwirt in Neuried.	1,2	Aufgelassen am 14.05.62 und eingetragen am 12.07.62. *(Klein) (Huber)*
2 a b	K l e i n Johann, Landwirt in Neuried, dessen Ehefrau Amalie,geb. Richter, ebenda, in Gütergemeinschaft.	1,2	Erbfolge lt.Erbschein des AG München vom 17.01.72 -VI 123/72- eingetragen am 03.03.72. *(Schmidt) (Maier)*
3	F u c h s Heinrich, Elektriker in Neuried.	1,2	Aufgelassen am 02.03.73 und eingetragen am 15.05.73. *Schmidt Maier*

Fig. 11.1 German register of title, inventory of property and proprietorship register (from Simpson 1976)

binders and ordered according to parcel numbers. This is sometimes opposed because of security reasons. But practical experience seems to show that there is little danger that a folio disappears or gets mixed up. It is always difficult to accommodate new material in bound books.

A loose-leaf system might well be of the type used in Kenya consisting of a folio about 30 cm wide by 15 cm long with the property and proprietorship section on one side and the encumbrances section on the other (see Fig. 11.2). The limited length of the folio and the type of binding make it possible to leave the lowest row with the parcel number and name of the first owner free and visible, the binder itself being more than twice as long as the folios which are inserted on successively lower levels. A folio is thus easy to find and one volume may contain almost 1000 folios. It is easy to insert a new folio or to exchange the old one for a new one which only shows current rights, while the old folio might be filed. There is in fact a general tendency to keep only current material in the register itself, while 'historical' material is stored in other ways. This tendency will become more and more pronounced along with the changeover to data processing.

An alternative to folios is index cards. The English registers, for example, are kept on index cards which are filed in drawers. Usually only cards with current information are kept there, while old cards are kept in the archive. This makes handling convenient, but also increases the risk of a card being lost or misfiled. There are many examples of such things happening, not least in developing countries, especially when the registers are open to public inspection.

As mentioned the parcels are filed in the register by number. It is also important, however, to be able to see how much land in one section or village is owned by each owner. An index of owners should, therefore, also be kept. This may be useful for assessment, agricultural and other statistics, for searches and also for checks on ownership and dealings in land.

In most registries, a daybook (an application book) is kept, showing the date and time when the application for registration was made. This may be helpful not only as a routine measure but also for dealing with questions of priority. The application and the attached deeds are assigned a number to which reference is later made in the register itself.

Normally, copies of the deeds are kept in the registry. Different systems can be used. In East African countries, for example, every registered unit is given a special file where deeds and other documents concerning the unit are collected. This is convenient at the early stages, but may cause trouble after a while unless the files are regularly scrutinized and old documents extracted, which of course makes a lot of work. It may be better to file the documents in chronological order as is generally done in Europe. Since the date of every deed affecting the register is shown in the register itself, it is very simple to trace a particular document with such a system.

Because of the danger of fire, etc., some kind of duplication of the register should be considered. In the case of a manual register, microfilming and other types of copying can be used if funds are available. Naturally these copies

EDITION_____
OPENED_____

PART I – DESCRIPTION OF PROPERTY

REGISTRATION SECTION	EASEMENTS, RESERVATIONS, ETC.	NATURE OF TITLE
PARCEL NO._____ APPROX. AREA _____ ACRES REGISTRY MAP SHEET NO._____		ABSOLUTE

PART II – PROPRIETORSHIP

ENTRY NO.	DATE	NAME OF REGISTERED PROPRIETOR	ADDRESS OR DESCRIPTION OF REGISTERED PROPRIETOR	CONSIDERATION	SIGNATURE OF REGISTRAR
		FIRST PROPRIETOR	SECTION	PARCEL NO.	

_____ TITLE NO.

PART II – PROPRIETORSHIP *(contd.)*

ENTRY NO.	DATE	NAME OF REGISTERED PROPRIETOR	ADDRESS OR DESCRIPTION OF REGISTERED PROPRIETOR	CONSIDERATION	SIGNATURE OF REGISTRAR

PART III – INCUMBRANCES

ENTRY NO.	DATE	NATURE OF INCUMBRANCE	FURTHER PARTICULARS	SIGNATURE OF REGISTRAR

Fig. 11.2 Register of title from Kenya

should be kept in a different place from the register itself, if possible in another building.

One method of duplication is to issue a certificate of ownership (or mortgage, etc.) to the owner. In the Torrens system the normal practice is to give the first owner a duplicate of the register folio at the first registration. Sometimes it is also required that this certificate be produced and transferred to the new owner when a transaction is made and registered.

There has been some discussion as to whether such certificates are essential or even desirable. It has rightly been pointed out (see, for example, Lawrance Mission 1966, p. 72) that it is the entry in the register and only that entry which proves title. A land certificate is merely evidence of that entry at the time the certificate was issued. The certificate should only be optional. It may, however, be useful both as a duplicate and as evidence to the owner that the matter has been settled. It is also helpful as a reference as it gives the official land unit number, which the owner might otherwise have trouble remembering. Certificates may also serve as a kind of propaganda for registration, and help to strengthen the feeling that registration is the natural way to protect rights in land.

11.3 Maintenance of the register

Discussions and studies concerning cadastre and land registration normally concentrate on the problems of establishing or radically improving a system. This is only natural as the initiation phase entails difficult decisions as well as heavy costs, and the success of a system will largely be determined by its design.

However, the value of a register is also heavily dependent upon its further maintenance. If it is not kept up to date, it quickly deteriorates in value. This is especially true of a registration system for legal titles. The most essential feature of such a system is that only registered titles are valid against a bona fide person. Without proper maintenance, the whole system will be jeopardized.

At the same time it must be admitted that it is not easy to keep a land register up to date. Strictly speaking, few developing countries have succeeded in doing so. Maintenance problems are also great for fiscal registers. Examples are easy to find – for example from the revenue surveys in India. But if tax collection is efficient, sooner or later it will be obvious that a change in ownership has occurred. Tax as such is, therefore, a strong correctional measure.

But maintenance problems are more difficult in the case of a legal land register, and this applies both to the short and the long term. The importance of the register may not be as obvious to the government as that of a record for tax determination and collection. And even if registration is intended to protect private land rights in general, the individual concerned may not understand the importance of registering a transfer. This is especially true in less-developed countries. Transfers there outside the family, mortgages, and other ways of using land as collateral have not yet become common. Land values are usually still rather low, even for bearing the costs of registration. Neither are credit opportunities very good in such cases. Things are likely to change with increasing population, general development and commercialization of land. But in the meantime steps must be taken to remove the obstacles that stand in the way of registration today, to make it more advantageous, and to ensure that changes are recorded. Some steps will be discussed below.

1. Registration should provide decisive advantages. One is that it gives security to rights. But in order that this can be the case, registration must be made compulsory, and be an absolute prerequisite for making a deed concerning land legally valid against a bona fide person. Registration should also constitute conclusive evidence that the person so registered is the holder of interest, and his rights should be guaranteed by the state. After the system has been introduced, registration should also be made a prerequisite for obtaining loans from banks and official institutions with land as collateral. This condition may also be extended to different kinds of subsidies.

2. Registration and related operations should be easy. This includes the writing of deeds for transfers and other land transactions. Local traditions may call for framing deeds in legalistic language and making them complicated and extensive, which makes legal assistance necessary. Experience from Australia, Kenya, etc., shows, however, that in most cases it is quite possible to use standard forms for different land transactions. As an example, according to the English Land Registration Rules of 1925, all the transferor has to do is to fill in the title number, the purchase price, and the name of the transferee before he himself signs the document (see Fig. 11.13). If he wants he can make alterations and additions. With such standard forms available, the only legal assistance which is needed in many cases is help from the registrar. Often the form is filled in by registry staff.

    Another way to make registration easier is decentralization. The applicants should not have to travel long distances to reach the registry office. On the other hand, small registration districts bring about problems in recruiting competent personnel. Some countries have tried to solve the problem by providing an officer to collect applications for registration in a local office on specified days of the week or month, while maintaining the registry itself in a district office.

    Further, registration can be simplified by concentrating all reporting to just one office. It is not unusual for a transferor to be required to visit the registrar as well as the revenue office or even the local government office. If the case concerns a subdivision, he may also have to make a special application for a survey of the lot. A better solution is to require the applicant to bring his case only to the land registry without further obli-

1. A transfer TO a company or corporation should, where necessary, follow form 3S.	⁽¹⁾ ⁽²⁾ **TRANSFER OF WHOLE** (Freehold or Leasehold)
2. Form 19 (Co.) is more convenient to use on a transfer BY a company or corporation.	(Rule 98 or 115, Land Registration Rules, 1925)

County or county borough or London borough ....**Greenwich**........

Title number.........**020376**........

Property........**2 Angel Park, Charlton**........

Date...**1st January**....19**68**. In consideration of....**Six Thousand**........

3. *Strike out if not required.*

pounds (£....**6000**........) ⁽³⁾ *the receipt whereof is hereby acknowledged*

4. *In BLOCK LETTERS, full name, postal address and description of the proprietor of the land.*

I, ⁽⁴⁾**WILLIAM SMITH of 645, REGENT STREET, LONDON W.1 JEWELLER**

5. *If desired or otherwise as the case may be (see rules 76 and 77.)*

6. *In BLOCK LETTERS, full name, postal address and description of the transferee for entry on the register.*

⁽⁵⁾ *as beneficial owner hereby transfer to :—*

⁽⁶⁾ **JAMES ROBINSON of 1620, OXFORD STREET LONDON W.1 MANUFACTURER**

7. *If there is not sufficient space for any special clauses they should be continued over the page ; the execution and attestation should then be added at the end.*

8. *A transfer for charitable uses should follow form 36 in the schedule to the Land Registration Rules, 1925 (see rules 121 and 122).*

the land comprised in the title above mentioned ⁽⁷⁾ ⁽⁸⁾

9. *If a certificate of value for the purposes of the Stamp Act, 1891, and amending Acts is not required, this paragraph should be deleted.*

It is hereby certified that the transaction hereby effected does not form part of a larger transaction or series of transactions in respect of which the amount or value or aggregate amount or value of the consideration exceeds £....**7000**.... ⁽⁹⁾

Signed, sealed and delivered by the said **WILLIAM SMITH**........

William Smith   (Seal)

in the presence of

Name....*Mary Jones*........

Address....*645 Regents Street, London W.1.*........

Description or occupation....*Jewellers Assistant.*........

The Solicitors' Law Stationery Society, Limited, 191–192 Fleet Street, E.C.4 ; 3 Bucklersbury, E.C.4 ; 49 Bedford Row, W.C.1 ; 6 Victoria Street, S.W.1 ; 15 Hanover Street, W.1 ; 55–59 Newhall Street, Birmingham 3 ; 31 Charles Street, Cardiff   CF1 4EA ; 19 & 21 North John Street, Liverpool, 2 ; 28–30 John Dalton Street, Manchester, 2.   **H**

March, 1968

Fig. 11.3 Form of transfer used for registration in England

gations. It is then the duty of the registrar to notify all the authorities concerned. In this way better co-ordination between different land records can also be secured. Last but not least, it is important that there is close co-operation between the registrar and the survey organization.

3. At the same time a system should be established by which the registrar is automatically informed of all transfers or successions handled by courts, notaries, local and central government authorities. This is especially important in the case of inheritance, as there is an obvious risk that changes in ownership will otherwise not be reported. Sometimes the system is augmented by a formal requirement that the registrar or the revenue officer make periodic field visits and enquiries to bring the records up to date. Controls on registration can be tightened by empowering the registrar to order registration in the case of non-compliance. Further checks can be introduced by means of a system for controlling transactions in land (to avoid extensive fragmentation, obstruction of planning regulations, etc.). Such systems exist in many European countries such as Sweden, and also in others like Kenya, where transactions must be approved by special authorities.

An additional, very important check is possible in countries which have records for periodic land taxes or other land charges. Since nobody wants to pay any unnecessary charges, such records are usually rather reliable and thus provide a valuable means of checking land registers. This is in fact a reason for introducing a land tax when a title registration system has been established in a country. Title registration not only provides prerequisites for land taxation but also increases the need for such a tax system.

4. The cost aspect is also important in this connection. Even if the first registration, if it is systematic, should be free of cost for the owners, it is natural that the appplicants bear some or all of the costs of later operating and maintaining the system. It is common practice to claim stamp duties in addition to registration fees. The duties are normally calculated as a certain percentage of the transaction value, and are sometimes very heavy. This is a questionable practice, especially in a poor country. It has been observed that when registration costs are high, people tend to avoid registering property, and the selling price reported in the deeds of transfer may be far below the actual price. This not only diminishes revenues for the government but also makes it difficult to obtain reliable price statistics as a basis for valuation. Registration fees and duties should, therefore, be fixed at a rather low level when title registration is introduced in a country. It may, after all, well be that the advantages of registration accrue more to the public than to the individual in the early stages.

In addition to costs, delays may obstruct the efficient maintenance of the land register. It is not unusual in developing countries for subdivisions to suffer long delays because of the lack of surveyors. The unique description of the land unit is an essential requisite of a title registration system, and resources for surveying must, therefore, be strengthened to meet the new needs when such a system is introduced.

It is important to understand that the matter of costs is not limited to registration fees, stamp duties and survey costs. The total cost of surveying, registration and building will be compared with corresponding costs for irregular development. The average man who wants to build a decent home for his family may well choose an alternative outside the institutional system rather than buy a lot within a planned area where requirements concerning survey, registration, building permission and building codes will increase his costs.

To conclude: proper maintenance is crucial for a land register. This requires education, personnel and material resources and well-developed routines. Active measures are also required to make registration more advantageous for the property owner, to diminish the difficulties and costs of the process and to develop different kinds of control measures. Generally, the establishment of several co-ordinated systems – such as cadastral records and land registers – facilitates keeping the total system up to date.

Maintaining a land registration system is, therefore, not a narrow, technical matter, but rather it is linked to institutional and organizational structure as well as to the education of experts, politicians and landowners. We shall consider a few of these aspects in Chapter 13. But first some special problems connected with adjudication and registration will be discussed in more detail than was possible in chapters 10 and 11.

12

Special problems

Three problems connected with land registration will be treated in this chapter:

- Individual or group registration
- Combined consolidation–registration
- Squatter rights.

12.1 Individual or group registration?

This problem has special significance in areas where customary land law prevails, such as in large parts of Africa south of the Sahara, in Polynesia, etc. (see, for example, Mifsud 1967 and Acquaye-Crocombe 1984). Under customary tenure, the ultimate or allodial rights to land are usually held corporately by a social group: a tribe, village, clan, lineage or family. Group-owned land is usually held in a fiduciary capacity by the head of the group on behalf of the whole group. But the head must act on the advice of other members, normally elders of the group. The land is rarely cultivated on a communal basis. The individual members of the group have distinct rights such as to build a house, grow crops, etc. The individual rights to the use of the land may or may not revert to the larger group if the land is abandoned. In customary tenure there are also usually restrictions against sales of land without the consent of the group.

Depending on the balance between group and individual interests, it may be preferable to register land on a group or individual basis or perhaps in both ways. This question has been discussed a great deal in the South Pacific area, and different solutions have been found. Group registration has been common. But in some places, such as in Tonga and in the independent states of Micronesia, individual registration has been chosen. The latter is, of course, a more expensive solution, but it may be appropriate where individual rights are strong. There are also problems connected with group registration. To quote Crocombe (1984 p. 36):

> The disadvantages of tying land to social groups now greatly outweigh its advantages in most cases. It reduces flexibility when greater flexibility is needed and this inhibits productivity. Two of the problems with group rights are to determine:
>
> 1. Who is, and who is not, a member of the group. This is not nearly as simple in practice as it may look in the theory. One may 'belong' by a number of criteria to various groups. And all criteria are negotiable and dependent on others. . . .
>
> 2. It mattered not only that you were a member of a group, but what kind of member you were. For example, the rights and obligations of a chief, an orphan, a wife, a son-in-law, a warrior, an absent sister, a talented cultivator, a refugee and various other statuses, differed greatly, even though all may be 'members' of the same group. We must get away from the notion that all members of a land holding group were equal.

In the Solomon Islands, the 1968 Land Settlement Ordinance left both possibilities open. The Act provides for individual ownership as well as joint ownership in a procedure for systematic adjudication. Joint owners are trustees and act on behalf of others, usually a group. They are supposed to consult the group and seek its consent before carrying out any land transactions. No more than five joint owners could be listed for any parcel of land. Public opinion in the Islands seemed to favour group registration.

The same might be said about Papua New Guinea. Very little adjudication of customary land has been carried out, and then mostly as group registration. According to the Commission of Inquiry into Land Matters 'individualization' should be approached cautiously. Where permanent crops are widespread, individual rights should be more clearly provided for in law and administration. Generally the commission recommended intermediate forms of tenure in which appropriate group rights are retained but sufficient rights are granted to individuals or sections of the group to enable them to use land to the best commercial advantage (Acquaye and Crocombe 1984, p. 54). The basic pattern of registration should be to register group titles, and make provision for the registered group to be able to grant rights of use in the form of registered occupation rights, leases and other subsidiary rights to individuals or sub-groups. The occupation right would be granted to the right holder for either a fixed term or indefinitely, and normally be heritable.

The above example from Papua New Guinea is an interesting attempt to work out a flexible system where customary rules and attitudes are largely retained while provisions are made for individual initiatives. As Crocombe points out, if a country with intensive land utilization registers land by groups, it will almost certainly have to provide for occupation rights, leases or other forms of individual rights within the group as well. Certain rules must then be followed, regulating time and conditions, heredity, whether or not rights can be granted to individuals outside the group or to absent members of the group, whether unused land shall revert to the group, maximum area, etc. Introducing registration in customary areas gives a unique opportunity to *define* rights even in those cases where registration is mainly a confirmation of earlier customary rules. Registration can thus provide a specific framework for existing rights and the future management of land, concerning both the physical boundaries of group or individual land and the rules governing the use of the land.

The choice between group or individual registration depends on the relative strength of group rights and individual rights. It also depends on political intentions. If established policy favours individual rights to land – because of a belief that this will increase productivity, establish a land market, etc. – then individual registration can be a powerful instrument as developments in Kenya have shown. The normal practice there is to register individual ownership, which has considerably hastened the process of individualization. On the other hand, the possibility of group ownership is also left open. The Land Adjudication Act of 1968 in Kenya explicitly states that any group which under customary law has exercised rights in or over land recognized as ownership shall be determined and registered as the owner of that land. The development of cattle production in the semi-arid range lands of Kenya has taken place almost entirely on land registered in the name of customary groups. Lawrance (1984, p. 3) gives other examples of group registration in Africa:

> In the Lilongwe Development Project in Malawi, land is initially brought onto the register in the name of the family head as 'family land', though provision exists for it to be sub-divided and transferred to individual owners with the agreement of the family and with the approval of the local land board. Provision is also made in Malawi for registration of customary land; land registered as 'customary land' may include *dambo*, i.e. swamp land used for communal grazing, sacred groves, village land and unallocated garden land, which may be allocated by the customary land authorities and registered in private individual ownership at some future date, but meanwhile continues to be administered by the traditional land authorities.

Technical and economic considerations may also influence the choice. In the case of group registration, the registered primary unit will not be the parcel but rather the area referred to the group (or possibly a homogeneous sub-unit of it). Group registration can thus radically diminish the number of registration units and thereby also the survey and registration costs. Rights of occupancy or leases to individuals can then be handled in an uncomplicated manner, perhaps by oral agreement according to customary rules, or by simple recording within the group. Such records may be successively improved, for example by sketching the individual parcels on an aerial photo. The important thing is that the system keeps initial investment costs low, while at the same time allowing for future improvements.

The following quotation from a research proposal (Larsson and Stoimenov 1985) may serve as an illustration of a situation where group registration (by villages) may be an appropriate solution for the first stage registration of land within customary areas:

During the seventies major changes occurred in the land settlement and land tenure in Tanzania caused by the programme of 'villagisation'. In principle all rural settlements should be concentrated to villages. According to the Act of 1975 the objectives of the establishment of villages are the transformation of individual and generally dispersed homesteads and farm units into clustered homesteads. Every village should contain not less than 250 family units and not more than 600 units. The suitable location of the village centre was settled by a local team. In the same time also new boundaries of the villages were decided. This total revolution of the existing settlement was to be implemented in a very short time – consequently there was no time for mapping and surveying of the villages. Demarcation and surveying of the new boundaries were left for later on.

In the New Agricultural Policy of Tanzania which was published in March 1983, the issues of land information, land tenure and title to land are given special weight as main reference points of the new policy ... A programme of land tenure and land use is outlined in which some of the main points are

- it is essential that all users of land feel confident that their investments of effort and money will be beneficial to them and their families

- few users have any documents showing their legal rights and legal duties, or even their boundaries which could give a rise to genuine disputes

- the Ministry of Lands, Housing and Urban Development will as soon as possible carry out a national survey of land use patterns and allocation. Village boundaries will be given priority.

This is a huge task for a country with more than 8000 villages and meager technical resources.

In a case like this, using the village as the unit of registration may be the best solution, because of the relatively low costs and because relationships within the villages are strong, and the village government has a decisive influence on allocation of the individual family plots. It should be possible, even with only internal village records, to give the occupants a strong sense of security, and to provide a basis on which credit institutions can grant loans.

Registration by groups is not only relevant in rural areas. Informal 'squatting' is increasing in urban areas in practically all developing countries. Methods must be found to give the squatters some security, while at the same time retaining some flexibility and making it possible to plan for successive improvement of the informal dwelling stock. One way might be to give formal title not to the individual settler but to a group within a squatting settlement. In much the same way as may be done in customary areas, the individuals are then given rights of occupancy for a shorter or longer period, subject to improvement of the dwellings. The system may well give the occupier enough security to stimulate investment and even to obtain bank credit, especially if the rights are stated in writing and the dwellings are given a unique number on an aerial photograph.

Even if individual tenure and registration is the most natural solution in most cases, it is not correct to state that registration of rights will automatically lead to the breakdown of old customary systems of group ownership.

The alternative of group registration should be seriously considered where conditions are suitable. If nothing is done, individualization will most probably take place where there is a growing pressure on land.

12.2 Combined consolidation-registration

Adjudication as such only fixes existing rights, and does not improve the general layout of the fields. However, adjudication and registration can be combined with structural measures. In some countries the adjudication authorities are given the power to straighten boundaries or improve them in other ways, to make reservations for common roads, canals, building sites for schools, etc. Some exchange of land between owners may also be included in the process.

In cases of very fragmented holdings, each consisting of many parcels, there may, however, be strong reasons for consolidating them into fewer blocks as a prerequisite for adjudication. We have earlier mentioned that, in the Central Province in Kenya, where fragmentation was very great, it was decided to start with consolidation. The fields of every owner were measured using simple methods, and the areas were calculated. A committee selected from among the owners and assisted by technical staff determined the layout of new lots. In the other provinces of Kenya, fragmentation was less pronounced, and adjudication and registration were mostly carried out without previous consolidation.

In some Western countries, too, consolidation has had to precede cadastral operations. Thus, in Switzerland, the normal procedure in fragmented areas lacking cadastres is to measure the old parcels using photogrammetric or graphic methods, carry out consolidation, demarcate and survey the new lots and then establish the cadastre, which also is used as a basis for the land register. Similar methods have previously been used in fragmented areas in Sweden. To hasten the registration procedure, however, it was decided to start with adjudication and title registration – carried out in a simple way and normally without any physical demarcation of the boundaries. Later, consolidation could commence when the area and the owners were prepared for it, and the necessary resources were at hand for expediting the proceedings.

There is no need to be dogmatic about whether registration or consolidation comes first. If it is felt that the need for consolidation is great, that the owners are prepared for it and that the resources are available, then it may be appropriate to start with consolidation. But if, on the other hand, it is considered more important that registration be given precedence, then it may be completed separately – preferably without much boundary demarcation. Consolidation can then be implemented at a later stage.

Some writers (Lawrance Mission 1966; Simpson 1967; West 1969) have argued forcefully that in cases of heavy fragmentation, adjudication and registration should be postponed until the owners are prepared to accept a prior consolidation. To quote the report of Lawrance Mission:

The act of registration of fragments may merely serve to freeze an unsatisfactory fragmented pattern of land holding. We can certainly see no possible justification in terms of agricultural development for registration of each fragment separately. It would impose survey problems of considerable magnitude, if fragments were small and numerous and would involve expenditure far in excess of the cost of any consolidation scheme so far undertaken in Kenya. If consolidation is both necessary and practicable, it should certainly be carried out before registration. We do not, of course, thereby suggest that consolidation can be carried out in the face of popular opposition. Acceptance by the majority of the people concerned is always essential, although the dissent of a small minority must not be allowed to hold up work. We strongly recommend, however, that where enquiries have revealed the need and practicability of consolidation, registration should be denied until the people concerned have agreed to prior consolidation.

This reasoning is quite acceptable if:

- the sense of ownership is rather weak, and registration, therefore, fixes a right that earlier was disputable ('freezes the pattern');

- precise methods of surveying and extensive demarcation are used even in cases of separate adjudication;

- the resources are sufficient to carry out both adjudication and consolidation within the required time.

A special case arises when adjudication is combined with irrigation, reclamation or settlement which are so radical in character that the total structure of the ownership pattern has to be changed. This is not unusual on customary lands. Ownership and other rights must be determined in such an area. In this case, adjudication must be combined with either an acquisition or a consolidation procedure, the latter keeping the present owners on the land but giving their farms a new structure.

12.3 Squatter rights

A frequently discussed question is how irregular occupation, 'squatting', should be dealt with in conjunction with adjudication and registration. Should it be accepted and the squatter be given secure title, a temporary right of occupancy or no rights at all? If title is granted, should it be absolute or limited and subject to certain conditions? In the latter case, should title become absolute only after a prescribed period of time, or contingent on cultivation, establishment of a building, etc.?

The problem may be different for first registration than for maintained registration.

First registration

In many – possibly most – countries there are specific rules in the land laws about *prescription*, whereby peaceable, public and uninterrupted possession without the permission of any lawful owner confers ownership after a specified period, for example 12 years. If the occupier can demonstrate that these conditions are fulfilled, he will be awarded full rights to the land as well as secured title in a registration proceeding.

But the problem is often more complicated. Some countries do not have any rules about prescription. Others make exception for state land, which is normally most subject to squatting. In customary areas there are seldom any distinct rules concerning land occupation without consent.

Policies may, therefore, need to be formulated about how to handle squatters in systematic adjudication and registration proceedings. Some points to consider are:

1. After systematic first registration has been completed in an area, in principle no unregulated rights should remain. Registration is also an opportunity to deal with irregular occupation where no prescription rights have developed. In such cases, insecure rights obviously hamper further investment and development.

2. In combination with adjudication of the area in question, it should, therefore, be decided which squatting units are acceptable and should be allowed to remain even though lacking legal rights. If state lands are involved, a grant or lease can be given. When the unit is acceptable, a grant is a natural solution in the long-term perspective as well. It will usually be conditional upon certain improvements being made within a prescribed period. If the conditions are fulfilled, the grant should develop into absolute title. A lease, on the other hand, may be used as a temporary solution in cases where the future existence of the land unit is doubtful, or where there is need for a 'check point' before full rights are given. Therefore, treatment of the unit should be determined more by planning considerations than by the duration of occupation.

3. This is especially true in urban areas. Many planners are opposed to granting secure rights to irregular settlers, fearing that this will inhibit future planned development. Such rights can certainly not be given to every settler or to every settlement area. But it must be possible to transform an existing irregular structure into a decent dwelling with simple roads and minimum standard facilities. Before any kind of rights can be granted to the squatters, a decision must, therefore, be taken concerning the suitability of the area for this type of development. If the area is deemed suitable, the essential features of the future infrastructure can be determined, and decisions taken about which dwellings must be removed for roads, etc. Special zoning regulations may be approved concerning acceptable building standards. Only then is it time for final adjudication

and registration. Depending on the situation, ownership rights or occupancy rights – possibly only lease rights – will be granted for longer or shorter duration. The adjudication and registration proceedings may be very simple, especially when only temporary rights are suitable.

In rural as well as urban areas, when a squatter does not have any legal prescription rights, it is necessary to consider the acceptability of the unit from the planning point of view. In rural areas these considerations may include the suitability of the site and the construction with regard to environmental protection, erosion dangers, forest preservation, etc. In urban areas it must be determined whether the irregular dwellings can be made to conform to desired land-use patterns in the short or long term. Such considerations will also determine which kind of rights the squatter should be given. In Thailand, for example, the occupier can be granted either a title deed or a certificate of utilization, giving evidence of possession. Once certain conditions are satisfied, such certificates can be converted to a full title deed (Williamson 1983).

Maintained registration

The squatter problem will not disappear after a system of title registration has been established. In countries with heavy population pressure in rural or urban areas, some settlement will probably continue to be irregular, even if the possibility of controlling squatting is greater within a title registration system.

A question which may be posed is if the legal rights of squatters will change when title registration has been introduced. It has often been argued that a squatter should not be able to obtain title by adverse possession against a registered proprietor. This was the position of the English land law until 1925 when the law was altered to recognize that registration of title should not affect the law of prescription and limitation (Simpson 1976, p. 153). Most of the Australian states originally followed the same course, but with the exception of New South Wales, they have now accepted provisions for the acquisition of title by possession.

However, other countries such as Malaysia have provided that possession should not give title to land adverse to the title of the registered proprietor regardless of the length of possession. Sometimes, special provisions are made for state land. In Thailand, for example, occupiers on government land do have possessory rights which are valid against other private individuals but not against the state. The legal position of a squatter on registered land thus depends on the provisions of the land law in that particular country. If possessory rights are accepted after the establishment of a title registration system, they can then be registered after the prescribed time has elapsed. Irrespective of this it is always possible to register the land if this is accepted by the registered owner. On private lands the property can be transferred by agreement, and on state lands a grant can be given if the location and size are acceptable.

The main way to solve the problems connected with continued squatting is, of course, to reduce the amount of irregular occupation. An efficient title registration system will provide better prerequisites for control, a more highly developed land market and greater opportunities as well as incentives to acquire and develop land in a regularized fashion. But as mentioned earlier, registration is only one means of preventing irregular occupation, and should be combined with other measures. Most important is that planned lots are available at a modest price or rent. The public sector should assume a certain amount of responsibility for land acquisition and for planning land development in advance before irregular occupation has begun to cause problems. It must also find ways to lower the costs of obtaining development and building permission. Low building standards may be accepted, at least in certain areas. If such measures are not taken, people with low incomes will not be able to afford the planned alternatives, and will still be forced to choose irregular occupation.

13

Organization, Automation, Education

This chapter will mainly deal with organizational questions and the organizational–technical problem of automation of cadastre/land register systems. Some aspects of the need for education within the sector will also be treated.

13.1 Organizational structure

The 1973 report by the Ad Hoc Group of Experts on Cadastral Surveying and Mapping discussed institutional organization as follows:

> The effective implementation of a cadastre is a complex operation involving the creation of a functional system of relationships among several institutions for the establishment, maintenance, use and future refinements of the cadastre. No part of the system is entirely independent of the other parts, and if one part fails to work, the system breaks down. The functions to be performed by the various offices concerned with a cadastre have already been described. It will be apparent from this description that:
>
> (a) There must be an office or offices in which information concerning legal rights and other information concerning parcels relevant to the particular purpose for which a cadastre is used will be registered and maintained.
>
> (b) There must be a survey organization responsible for the production and maintenance of the cadastral maps and the description and numbering of parcels; this organization might also collect, if feasible, other information required on such subjects as land use or buildings.
>
> Ideally the registration and survey functions described above should be performed by a single agency. This arrangement guarantees the best possible co-ordination between the various parts of the whole operation. However, in many countries there already exist different agencies, sometimes established by law, which are charged with performing different aspects of the activities involved in establishing a

cadastre; or there may be several agencies in one country each charged with establishing cadastres for particular purposes. These agencies may already have collected at least part of the information needed for a new cadastre and this work must therefore be correlated with that of any new agency. In practice it will be difficult to alter existing arrangements of this kind, for which there may be historical or political reasons.

There is no single arrangement for co-ordinating these different functions. Experience shows that many different organizational structures may lead to satisfactory operations. In The Netherlands, for example, cadastral and land registration functions are performed within the same office and closely co-ordinated. But in most other countries the cadastral and registration functions are separated. The former may be connected to the revenue authorities, which was a natural solution in the days when the main purpose of a cadastre was to determine land tax. But the cadastral function may also be the responsibility of a separate survey authority. In countries such as Denmark and Switzerland, the actual surveying is performed by private surveyors while the cadastre itself is a government responsibility. In other countries, like Germany and Austria, the whole organization is governmental.

These examples show that cadastre/land registration can be organized in very different ways, while still, as it appears, operating efficiently. Much depends on the pre-existing institutional framework. For this reason, existing organizations should not be altered radically when more general and improved systems of cadastre/land registration – or for that matter refined land information systems – are introduced. If one authority has previously been responsible for some type of record or land information, it normally should continue to have this responsibility. The implementation of reforms should disturb existing institutional structures as little as possible. Too much turbulence in existing operations may create irritation and rivalry and hamper future co-operation.

On the other hand it must be recognized that new tasks may require some new structures. This may provide the opportunity to establish a new agency with – if possible – young and energetic people, who can be charged with monitoring and co-ordinating the whole process.

An example is the establishment in Kenya of a new Adjudication Department in conjunction with the introduction of land registration for customary land. Adjudication was something new, but at the same time the very heart of the process. The Survey, Lands and Registration Departments could continue working on their old tasks while also assuming new ones. But the main responsibility for control, stimulation, information and co-ordination of the whole process was placed on the Adjudication Department.

Another example may be taken from Sweden. When it was decided to automate the cadastre and land register, and at the same time to establish a joint information system with revenue registers, population registers, etc., the task was not assigned to any existing authority. A new organization was established – the Central Register for Real Estate Data. The existing organizations continued their operations, maintaining cadastres, land registers, etc.

But supervising the conversion from manual registers to databases, developing systems and co-ordinating the different activities are mainly the responsibility of the new organization.

There *may* be risks involved in dividing the work among different institutions, but it *need* not lead to fragmentation of efforts provided that certain conditions are fulfilled. Let us list some favourable factors for a well-functioning system:

- *One* organization is given primary responsibility for working out rules governing the new system and co-ordinating the work of various offices involved in monitoring the project.

- All duplication is avoided. It is clearly stipulated *who* is responsible for *what* information. Well-defined channels of communication are established as are fixed routines for the exchange of data among different departments and records.

- All data are designed for multipurpose use rather than for use within one department.

- Land units are assigned *one* identification code which is used in all public and private records. In case of automation, this code can be used as a key for integrating different records.

- The structure is user friendly and stimulates the flow of relevant data into the system. This means that service offices are decentralized in cases where direct contacts are necessary between citizens and authorities.

Beyond this, it is difficult to make general recommendations concerning a suitable institutional structure for the cadastral/land registration sector as part of the overall land information sector. So much depends on the existing organization and earlier developments. New technology can also change the situation, as expressed by Morgan (1985):

> New technologies evoke changes in the supporting organisational structure. Institutional reform is an important prerequisite to the successful application of most L.I.S. technologies. To maximise the potential of many technical capabilities, system designers will need to provide user training, develop a corporate data sharing infrastructure, organise funding, redefine traditional responsibilities, and overcome historical encumbrances.

One such technology, which may change structures is widespread use of automatic data processing. We will now consider this subject in relation to cadastre/land registration.

13.2 Automation

The very nature of land records such as cadastre and legal land registers makes automation a natural development. As Simpson (1976) expresses it:

The operation of a land registry is basically an exercise in filing the indexing and storing of particulars in respect of each land parcel in such a way that they can be amended, retrieved, and presented without delay or mistake. It seems inevitable, therefore, that sooner or later the computer, the miraculous device which has been developed for this sort of purpose, will be used.

Today, work is going on in practically all industrialized countries concerning the use of electronic data processing (EDP) in these connections. In Chapter 9 we discussed how EDP methods have been introduced in surveying and mapping as well as in the storing of survey records and data.

Cadastral records and land registers are gradually automated, too. This is done not only to make the handling of the records more efficient but also to link cadastral/land register data more conveniently to other land-related data, thus establishing an important component in a land information system. As discussed earlier, large-scale maps and cadastral information are the foundation of parcel-based land information systems – 'multipurpose cadastres' – as shown in Fig. 13.1.

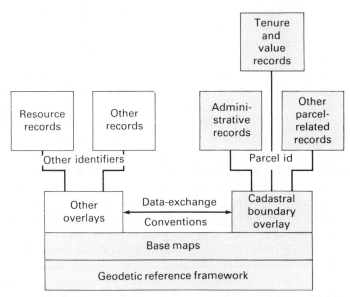

Fig. 13.1 Multipurpose cadastre components (based on National Research Council 1980)

There are many alternative systems to solve this problem. It is still too early to say which is the best. Naturally, the solution will also much depend on the whole structure of cadastral and land registration records and the ambition the country has to build on them for a more general land information system. Because of this and because a principle of this study has been not to go into any depth concerning technical solutions, we will just give examples of solutions in a few countries.

The Swedish system has been briefly described already in Section 4.2. It is based on a central data bank with different bases (Andersson 1980): one base for primary identifiers such as property designations, addresses and block names; one for data concerning such properties as cadastral and land register data as well as co-ordinates; one for physical plans and regulations of land use, etc. Further additions are discussed such as building data. The basic input is of two kinds: data concerning the cadastral units and data related to titles and rights. Both are guaranteed by the government. The printed cadastre and land register have disappeared.

The system is an on-line system, that is, direct dialogue is possible between user and computer. Every regional survey organization or land registrar is equipped with a communication terminal with both visual display and print-out facilities. When registration or re-registration is called for, for example because of a change in ownership, the registrar consults the land data bank through the terminal and obtains the present data for the cadastral unit in question. The registrar then makes the required changes and obtains a control card printed out by the terminal. After checking he sends the data bank a confirmation, the bank prints out the official documents – ownership certificates and so on – and communicates the changes to other relevant authorities and records. In this way an applicant can request registration one day and obtain this document two days later.

The public will still have access to the files at the offices of the registrars, and will also have access via the terminals to every property unit in the country. Banks, insurance companies, institutions and private persons may access the system via their own terminals. The land data bank is integrated with other important national registers such as registers of land-use plans, population, assessment, etc., using parcel number or address as identification key. As the land data bank contains the central co-ordinate for every cadastral unit, all register information on persons, buildings, households, enterprises, real estate, transfers and purchase prices, development plans, assessed values, taxable income, etc., can be positioned and mapped automatically. The system and its use are described in more detail in Appendix B, which also provides additional information on the above-mentioned project to develop a land information system in the Maritime provinces of Canada.

In a few other countries, similar systems are operational – for example in Austria (Hoeflinger 1986, 1990). In many other countries they are planned: Australia, New Zealand, United Kingdom, Germany, etc. (see Hesse and Williamson 1990; Robertson 1990; Smith 1990; Schenk 1990). There are also examples of a decentralized organization. Denmark thus keeps a central cadastre comprising a register of the nation's real properties and a system of maps with boundaries and numbers (Stubkjaer 1981), which also contains data of areas and restrictive conditions pursuant to agricultural and forestry legislation. This is now in the process of automation. But there also exist computerized registers of land units in the country's 275 municipalities, used as an information source and also as the basis of valuation and tax assessment, together with a building and housing register.

Norway is also developing an information system – the GAB system – distributed to eight regional IBM-equipped data centres (see Fig. 13.2 (Onsrud 1984)). It contains data on 2.3 million properties and their owners, 1 million addresses and all buildings constructed since 1983. GAB is a pure information system and does not have the legal force of a register of titles. The municipalities and the local court offices report either directly on-line to the data bank, or by written forms to a government office on the county level, where the forms are digitized. GAB is an open system to be used by both public and private organizations.

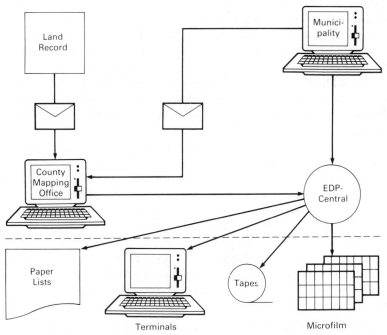

Fig. 13.2 Regional data distribution process in Norway (Onsrud 1984)

The systems mentioned above have contained millions of land units. In a developing country, the number of registered land units is often comparatively small, as the records normally cover only a part of all the property in the country. Simpler solutions are then possible (among those who have discussed appropriate systems in developing countries may be mentioned Bogaerts 1985; Henssen 1981; Holstein 1987; Larsson 1971; Lawrance 1985; Simpson 1976; West 1969). An example can be taken from Zambia, where existing records have been transferred to micro-computers. Important objectives of the programme were to reduce duplication in the storage of information, improve the collection of ground rent, plan for an expected increase in the registration of titles, get rid of registers that were in tatters or badly torn and make it possible to compile information. The condition in the lands and deeds register was such that much time was spent on looking for files or other information. Things were becoming chaotic. A decision was taken to computerize the property records kept in the Survey Department, as well as the revenue records and lands and deeds register within the Lands Department. All these records should be stored in the same computer, but the responsibility for maintenance of the records is strictly divided between the departments. The three registers will be cross-run and comparative corrections and completions will be made. It is hoped that this will not only give a correct content in the records, improve land management considerably and raise more income from revenue but also reveal the occurrence of vacant, not utilized land.

Many more examples of different types of automation could be given, as work on such systems is performed in most Western countries. But what is said is enough to demonstrate that many alternatives can be discussed. Automation has usually started with the cadastre, but so far there are few examples of the integration between cadastre and legal land registers which we found in Sweden. Studies in Sweden show that the most obvious benefits seem to be anticipated by also automating the land register and the handling of certificates of title, etc.

The development in many countries is also progressing in this general direction. It is greatly stimulated by the possibilities of integrating cadastres and land registers with other systems: of making them the core of parcel-based land information systems. Automation greatly increases the value of cadastral information, and provides a solid basis for establishing a 'multipurpose' cadastre. This concept does not refer to *one* register with attached maps, but to a whole system of interconnected databases, which can be developed in stages, and which do not necessarily need to be centralized, but can include networks of personal computers. To cite the United Nations 1985 Ad Hoc Group of Experts on Cadastral Surveying and Land Information Systems:

> The development of computer and information technology is taking over many manual tasks and in spite of the high capital outlay, can offer significant reductions in cost. The most expensive and time consuming part of a computerized land information system is the collection and conversion of data. A trend towards decentralization and deconcentration, with smaller dedicated systems linked together to form a larger overall system is seen. To provide that linkage, standards for the interchange of data must be established and a common spatial referencing system enforced. Effective co-operation and co-ordination among agencies is essential.

Figure 13.3 shows how such links can be established between different databases and agencies to form a co-ordinated system with the cadastral and land registration data as important foundation stones. Automation is essential for constructing such systems.

Another important step is *digitization* of cadastral maps and other basic data, which makes it possible to combine map information with other spatially related information, to change the scale and mode of presentation

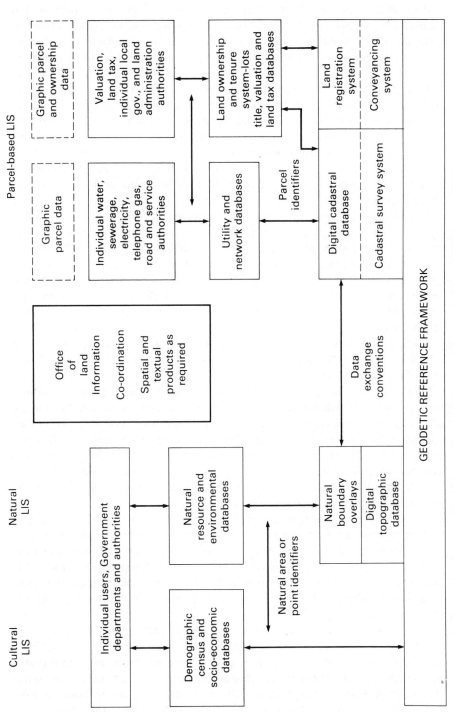

Fig. 13.3 Functional model for the South Australian land information system (from Williamson 1986)

and to let the machine do the drawing. A further important feature is that digitization makes it easy to delete and add data and thus keep the maps up to date. Another essential aspect of digitization is the possibility of selecting different 'layers' of information from different sources and combining them in the most suitable way for the purpose in question (see Fig.13.4).

Digital map data are normally processed either as vector or raster data. In the former, points are represented by their co-ordinate values, lines by strings of co-ordinates and areas by perimeters or representative points. In the case of raster data, a map, aerial photograph or the like is scanned as if overlaid by a grid, with each square being assigned a numerical value, for example in tones ranging from black to white. Raster scanning is a quick and automatic process, but it generates a very large volume of data and often results in less precise images.

Vector co-ordinates may be acquired through direct field surveys or as a by-product when mapping from aerial photographs, but generally, they are obtained by manual methods using digitizing tables. A digitizing table usually has an orthogonal net of embedded wires, which are sensed by a cursor as it passes overhead. The resulting electrical impulses are converted into measurements of the position of the cursor on the table. (see Dale and McLaughlin 1988, for a more detailed presentation of different methods and techniques).

Should these automation methods also be used when introducing a new or improved cadastral/land registration system in developing countries? There are different opinions on this question.

Changing a registration system is a complicated affair, and so is automation. Doing both simultaneously may well be too risky. Adequate knowledge about land registration and large, computerized information systems is often lacking in these countries, as is the ability to afford capital-intensive systems. As Doebele (1985) pointed out: '... attempts to install fully articulated systems from the start have, like fully developed public housing, tended to bog down into ineffectiveness when confronted with the magnitude of the problem and the high expense of processing each unit.'

It may be better to start by establishing a manual cadastral/land registration system in some key provinces, and trying hard to make it work efficiently. After that it may be time to consider some kind of computerization as a next step. If, however, a title registration system already exists for parts of the property in a country and essentially will be kept, immediate automation may be a realistic alternative. The example given from Zambia may be valid for many countries.

In the long run most countries will certainly take the step of introducing EDP in land registration. When a new or improved system of cadastre/land register is established in a country it must, therefore, be so organized that it will be easy to switch over to an automatic system at a later stage. Sometimes this stage will arrive very quickly. It is essential for future costs to take automation into account from the very start, and to prepare the system for it. Because, as is stated by the 1985 Ad Hoc Group of Experts on Cadastral

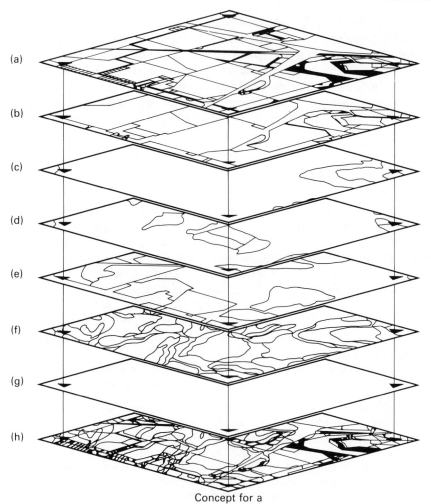

Concept for a
Multipurpose Land Information System
Section 22, T8N, R9E, Town of Westport, Dane County, Wisconsin

(a) Parcels   Surveyor, Dane County Lane Regulation and Records
                          Department.
(b) Zoning   Zoning Administrator, Dane County Land Regulation and
                          Records Department.
(c) Floodplains   Zoning Administrator, Dane County Land Regulation and
                          Records Department.
(d) Wetlands   Wisconsin Department of Natural Resources.
(e) Land Cover   Dane County Land Conservation Committee.
(f) Soils   United States Department of Agriculture, Soil Conservation
                          Service.
(g) Reference Framework Public Land Survey System corners with geodetic
                          coordinates.
(h) Composite Overlay   Layers integrated as needed, example shows parcels, soils
                          and reference framework.

Fig. 13.4 Example of layers of information in the Dane County project (fron Chrisman *et al.* 1986)

Surveying and Land Information Systems: 'The most expensive and time-consuming part of a computerized land information system is often in the data collection or its conversion into computer-readable form. The process of transcribing all the manual records into a form in which they are error-free and can be read by the computer may take at least a decade.' If the manual records are adapted for computer use from the start, this transition time can be substantially shortened.

13.3 Training and education

In many countries, especially developing ones, there is little practical experience and knowledge concerning modern methods of cadastral survey and cadastral/land registration systems. Recent decades have seen extremely rapid developments in photogrammetry, instruments, electronic methods of surveying, computerized mapping, digital data processing, etc. Progress has been slower in the field of cadastral and land registration records, but computerization is now changing the picture. Even traditional title registration systems and systematic adjudication methods have been unfamiliar in many countries. To conclude, there is a great need of information, training and education in these fields.

Information and education should be understood in a broad sense. According to the United Nations 1973 Ad Hoc Group of Experts:

> In a broader sense, everyone upon whom the cadastre will impinge should receive some form of training or orientation. The principal groups are: high-level policy-makers; professional personnel; technical and subprofessional personnel; the general public (property owners); and relevant government agencies which will use the cadastre. Training requirements are so varied from country to country that little useful information of general nature can be given. Nevertheless, there are some demands for training, common to developing countries, to which international bodies and countries having technical assistance programmes could address their attention:
>
> (a) High-level policy-makers in developing countries sometimes require short-term intensive training in the fundamental aspects of cadastres, particularly when a country is about to initiate a cadastral programme. This demand could best be satisfied by periodical regional seminars;
>
> (b) High-level administrative and professional staff could benefit by observation of cadastral programmes in effective operation in other countries in order to adapt procedures and techniques to their own local circumstances;
>
> (c) Professional personnel should also have the opportunity to receive mid-career training for the purpose of broadening their outlook and keeping up to date on modern developments in their fields by means of periodical seminars in particular disciplines;
>
> (d) The general public must, of course, be reached through mass media.

There are some international courses especially designed for people from developing countries (such as courses at ITC, Holland, Polytechnic of East

London and the National Survey of Sweden in co-operation with the Central Board of Real Estate Data). Their lengths vary from ten months to less than two months. All are oriented towards target groups (b) and (c) above, and they deal primarily with land law, cadastral surveys, land registration and general aspects of land information systems and computerization. They serve people who have already developed expertise in one particular field. The land information managers may come from a variety of backgrounds such as surveying, land registration, land law and administration, computer science, etc.

Such courses are valuable for developing basic knowledge of problems and techniques in this field among upper and middle administrative and professional staff from countries lacking solid experience of modern methods. They can be especially useful in conjunction with the introduction of new or improved systems. In the long run, however, the essential training and education must be organized within the country itself.

One way is through 'on the job' training. Even if foreign aid is available, the actual operations must of necessity be commenced on a limited scale, in the form of pilot projects, and then gradually extended when experience has been gained and sufficient personnel have been trained. The training programme as such may include supplementary courses for personnel with ample experience of older methods, but it will consist primarily of closely supervised practical work and instruction in the field within a few districts. The first trainees can then take over the practical training of new officers.

Parallel to the field training, theoretical courses should be developed on different levels, and designed for several different target groups. Surveyors with a mainly technical background need further education, not only in suitable cadastral survey methods such as the use of photogrammetry and photo-interpretation, but also in legal and institutional matters. The initial recording of ownership and other rights is often made in connection with the survey. The survey officer should, therefore, have some knowledge of the legal rules concerning rights to land. Many surveyors will also administer both surveying and adjudication operations. They should, therefore, be provided with some background on the motives for, and the characteristic features of, land registration as such.

The adjudication officer may have a surveying, Civil Service or legal background, and his further training should be determined on this basis. As he may be given the power to decide cases in the first instance, he should have adequate legal and administrative knowledge, as well as some knowledge of surveying, both for determining boundaries and for administering the entire operation.

Further training is needed for registration officers, too. Keeping a register of titles is rather different from keeping a register of deeds. The registrar must now scrutinize the documents, and is not allowed to register any transfer or any new right in land until he is satisfied that all legal conditions have been observed. This requires legal training. If the register is to be computerized, training in the use of computerized registers will also be needed.

Thus, there is a wide spectrum of training and educational needs. It is vital that this be taken into account from the start, and that planning and training programmes commence as early as possible. The speed of the adjudication and registration work in a country depends, in the first instance, more on capable personnel than on any other resource.

14

Progressive systems: ways of simplification

14.1 Progressive systems

The analysis in the previous chapters has dealt mainly with the problems of establishing comprehensive, multipurpose cadastral/land registration systems, in the belief that a fragmentary or limited system has little to recommend it. A comprehensive system offers so many advantages and opens so many more possibilities that it generally is preferable in the long run.

However, when there is a lack of resources, simplified solutions may be necessary as a starting point. As in many other cases, systems from the industrialized world cannot be transplanted *in toto* to developing countries, but must be adapted to meagre resources and other conditions. To cite Williamson (1986): 'Care must be taken not to promote a system which is beyond the reach of these countries. Virtually by definition, developing countries are poor countries. While the multipurpose concept is desirable, it is still an ideal. Many countries cannot even afford a most rudimentary deeds system without any map base, let alone a comprehensive land information system.'

Doebele (1985) supports the concept of 'a "progressive" cadastral system, that is a system that can be applied rapidly, upgraded and improved to conventional standards as rapidly as resources and political support permit'. This means, *inter alia*, that when a new or improved system is introduced in a country short on resources, the system may be technically simple but should nevertheless be not only of sound design but also readily adaptable to further modernization. It also means that the road from simple to more developed systems should be *rational*, that is, progress shall not render earlier work useless. Within the same general framework, it should be possible to add new types of information or qualitatively better information step by step when resources permit. In such a case, several kinds of simplification may be possible in the first phase.

We have already touched upon many possible means of making the initial introduction of the system less expensive. In this chapter, however, we shall treat these possibilities in a more systematic way, even if this necessitates some repetition. Our main question is this: which kinds of initial simplification can be accepted without hampering future development?

The discussion will concentrate on the following measures:

- Reduction of functions
- Block units
- Limited boundary delimitation
- Simplified survey
- Minimized field work
- Provisional registers
- Selectivity

14.2 Reduction of functions

A comprehensive land record system is desirable from many viewpoints. It will provide all the benefits discussed in Chapters 6 and 7 only when it can meet the needs of general land information, taxation, the guarantee of land rights, land management and land control. However, such comprehensiveness may have to be a long-term goal. If an immediate shortage of resources requires a reduction in the number of functions the system can serve, which essential functions ought to be retained?

The primary basis for even the simplest records – necessary for future development – is obviously a systematic division into land units. If the principles for such a division are set out so that they can be used all over the country for all the main types of land records, the division into land units can gradually be expanded, new units can be added, and new records can be included in the future within the same common frame. To reach this end the division should be

- *hierarchical*, that is, structured on different levels and go from district to block to sub-block and to unit designation within the sub-block. Some countries do not have a well-developed structure of this type. In Zambia, for example, all new units are numbered in running order all over the country regardless of their location;
- *flexible*, that is, employ logical and simple rules for making changes of designation when a unit is subdivided, amalgamated, or otherwise

changed. Even several successive changes should not lead to complicated unit designations;

- *unique*, that is, no two units shall ever have the same designation;

- *multipurpose*, that is, be suitable for use – singly or in combination with other units – in all types of land records and tasks irrespective of the purpose (general information, taxation, property rights, etc.)

It is a further advantage if the land units are basically stable and seldom change. Units based on short-term leases or temporary owners are, therefore, less convenient.

Historically the initial step towards systematic land records has been some designation of the primary taxation unit or the primary tenure unit, sometimes based on large-scale maps, sometimes not. Because the designations of the land units have not always satisfied the conditions above, problems have often emerged when the number of units has increased or when efforts have been made to integrate other records into the same system.

Even if, therefore, the system in the initial stage is intended only for information or only for taxation, a division into carefully structured land units is necessary as an essential basis for later development. Further information – areas, land uses, assessed values, owners, other rights in land, buildings, prices, and so on – can be added to this framework either from the start or later on. A sound initial structure makes it possible to add new functions when needed and when resources become available. With added and increasingly accurate information, the system can fill additional functions, and gradually develop a multipurpose use. Especially in cases where a comprehensive system involves substantial and difficult legal changes, this approach best paves the way for future progress.

14.3 Block units

The initial work of establishing a record system is very much dependent on the number of land units. A radical way of reducing the number is just to record the blocks – the villages, the wards, the family units, or whatever the natural group is – but not the individual unit of ownership or occupancy.

In Chapter 12 we discussed different aspects of group registration, noting there that it may be motivated by the type of tenure, tradition, customary law, etc. Clearly, group registration offers the important and obvious advantages of less work and less expense. However, where strong rights of individual tenure exist, it also means a considerable reduction in function. Group registration does not provide information about the individual lots, their areas and values, or existing rights in the lots. It cannot grant full and guaranteed security to the occupier, nor does it make it possible to obtain bank loans with land as collateral.

On the other hand, group registration can be a first step, and one which will not hamper the later registration of individual titles. Even this later registration may be established step by step. It can start as a private record of members' rights to group land kept by the group representatives. If there are rights of occupancy to individual lots, this record may include a description of location, which can even be noted on aerial photographs when available. At some stage, when the institutional and technical conditions are ripe, these internal records may be transferred through legal proceedings to official land records with individual titles. This does not need to be done simultaneously for all groups. The transfer should instead be determined by the conditions and wishes of each group. Registration of blocks only is, therefore, one possible way to reduce work without preventing the development of recognized individual titles.

14.4   Limited boundary delimitation

The most demanding aspect of establishing a cadastre or land register is the determination, demarcation, and surveying of the boundaries of each unit. It may be advisable to consider how to establish useful land records with simple methods of delimitation and demarcation.

In our earlier discussion of some of these methods, we noted how they can be facilitated by the legal concept of 'general boundaries.' Help from the occupier himself in determining and demarcating the boundaries will also mean less time and smaller public outlays for the operations. Willingness to accept as sufficient simple boundary demarcations such as hedges, ditches, earth ridges, fences, etc., can further lower the costs.

Sometimes it is even possible to establish useful records without any determination of the boundaries. We shall cite one example. When, a few decades ago, the World Bank and the Tanzanian Government decided to upgrade certain parts of Dar-es-Salaam, the programme included measures to give the squatters more secure rights to their homes, and thus stimulate investments in buildings. Simple methods were used. All dwellings were numbered on aerial photographs. Using these numbers as identifiers, records of all accepted squatter units were established. The squatters' rights were defined in mutual contracts, which, however, did not include any specific description of boundaries. Therefore, even if such records cannot provide precise knowledge of the exact boundaries, they can still support the right to stay in a location for a given period and thus stimulate further improvements while also making possible outside loans with land as collateral. In the Tanzanian case, the records were not included in the official registration system, but theoretically they could be if the rules of registration were adapted to include such methods. In any case, such simple, provisional registers can serve as the basis for the subsequent development of a final register if the designation of the land units follows the general registration structure from the start (see Fig. 14.1).

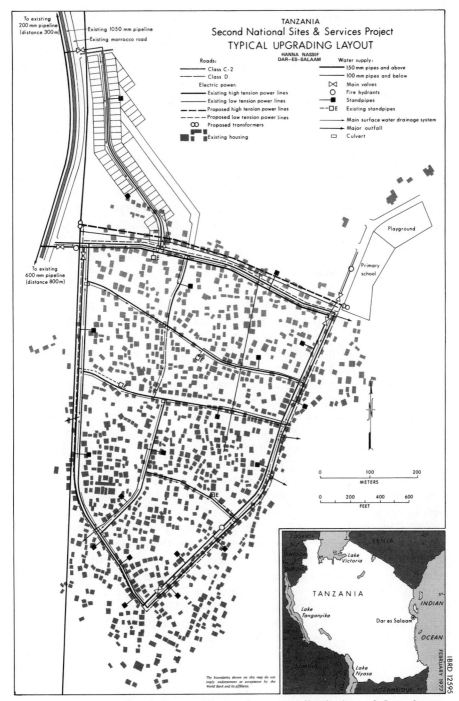

Fig. 14.1 A squatter area in Dar-es-Salaam where upgrading is planned. Some houses have to be removed for roads and watercourses. The others are given unique identification numbers and certificates of occupancy for a specified number of years. No individual boundary lines are determined

14.5 Simplified survey

The possibility of using simplified survey methods for the initial adjudication and registration have been discussed at length in Chapter 9. We need only stress here that there are no strict standards of accuracy for cadastral or land registration surveys. Because balancing the advantages of greater accuracy against higher costs and available resources is a matter of judgement, a flexible attitude is necessary. The required accuracy should never be determined primarily by standards used in other – perhaps more developed – countries or by a desire for technical perfection. For example, it is not unusual for efficient photogrammetric methods to be ruled out in cadastral surveying because of old regulations prescribing ground survey methods. Survey costs represent such great expenditures that the methods used should never be determined by tradition or outdated regulations.

14.6 Minimized field work

As costs for field work are normally rather high, it is important, when attempting to simplify cadastral/land registration methods and to minimize work, to consider using what is already available. *One way* is to use older, existing maps and records as far as possible to arrive at a skeleton parcel/ownership system. Since a system developed in this manner will usually be incomplete and of uneven quality, further field studies will be necessary. But these too can be kept to a minimum by compiling data in the office to develop the general structure of the real-estate system. However, if unrealistically high standards are applied to the contents of maps and records, such measures become much less practicable.

Another way is to use photogrammetry as much as possible, both to interpret boundary systems in the office and to lessen the field work. As has been noted, this makes lower costs likely and can also speed up the operations significantly.

These two methods can often be effectively combined. Photogrammetric methods can be used to densify the control grid thus providing a better basis for compiling whole map-sheets from older maps. Furthermore, if the boundaries are visible in aerial photos, these maps can more easily be fitted together so that the boundaries can be adjusted and completed according to the pictures. Several European countries, as well as some of the Australian states, have used this combination of methods to produce cadastre/register map-sheets instead of isolated 'island' maps.

14.7 Provisional registers

Even if the final goal is to obtain a reliable title register, it may be easier to start with provisional registers. This means that the register does not provide any formal guarantee, but it does provide provisional evidence of title. This diminishes the demand for thorough title searches and lengthy and costly legal proceedings. This method can also be used for specific land units where it is difficult to show an unbroken chain of ownership transfers, or where the claimant has not been in peaceable possession of the land long enough to establish full title.

If the provisional titles are unchallenged for several years, their validity will gradually increase. Time will do the same work as more costly investigations or a more complicated appeals system. After the legally prescribed number of years, the unchallenged, provisional titles can automatically become final and absolute, with full guarantees. In this way the final goal can be reached using only a simplified adjudication and registration proceeding.

14.8 Selectivity

Selectivity in establishing a cadastral/land registration system means that by restricting the proceeding to a selection of land units, the costs can be matched to calculated benefits and to the resources of the country. If the selection is made judiciously, the impact on the economy, etc., will be relatively significant even if the number of selected parcels is small.

Selection can be made along different lines. One is *individual* selection, according to either voluntary or compulsory registration. In the first case the landowner himself applies and pays for registration as well as for surveying, if needed. In the second case registration is required under certain specific conditions, such as transfer (as in England) or a grant from the state. Voluntary registration and grant registration are the most common methods in the Third World. They are cheap for the government but expensive for society because of the need to survey individual units. Therefore, if the goal is to develop a multipurpose cadastral/land registration system, this method is not very efficient. However, it may be justified as a starting point for future development, and is sometimes the only method the country can afford at the time.

Another method is *area* selection. This is an integral part of systematic adjudication/registration, which can never be implemented immediately but must proceed area by area according to a system of priorities. Some of the factors determining such a system were discussed in Section 8.7. We will stress here only the fact that selection implies that different methods and different rules may be applied in different parts of a country or for different types of real estate. Thus selection opens up the possibility of a flexible approach to system development, a flexibility which should be used to get the maximum results from the minimum outlay. Selectivity also makes it possible to adapt the process to existing resources.

14.9 Axes of variation

To summarize: progressive cadastral/land registration systems can begin on very different levels with very different costs. The possible types of simplification can be seen as variations along a number of axes, which together determine the information content and the standard of the whole system. The most important axes are the following:

1. *The land-unit division axis.* For all parcel-based systems, a division and indexing in land units is imperative as this is the very foundation of such systems. But variations can be found in the size of the units – group (village), farm, parcel, etc.

2. *The location-determination axis.* The location can be indicated without maps as was done in the Domesday Book and in most ancient tax records. It can also be indicated by a point on an aerial photograph or a map, or as a co-ordinate. If the boundaries of the units have been determined on the ground, they can be recorded in a map or co-ordinate record with a varying degree of accuracy, partly depending on whether ground survey, photo-interpretation or photogrammetrical methods are used. Great variations in methods and results are possible; normally this axis is the one which has the greatest influence on the total costs.

3. *The information-content axis.* To the primary land unit designation can be added various information connected to this unit such as area, land use, buildings, assessed value, owner, other rights, population, etc. Some of it may be contained in property/cadastral records, some in land registers and some in other registers connected to the system by common identifiers. The system can be further extended by secondary records kept for local or private use and joined to the system by the same identification keys. Thus there is a very wide scope of variations along this axis.

4. *The information-quality axis.* Practically all information included in a system of land records can vary considerably in quality. The matter of quality must be seriously discussed when making decisions about a new or improved system. Naturally, one must consider not only the requirements for reaching a certain standard but also the costs and the practical possibility of reaching it. As discussed above, the quality can sometimes increase automatically with time (provisional titles become absolute titles) in which case it may be advantageous to be satisfied with the lower level initially. Irrespective of which level is chosen at the start, this should be clearly expressed, since a quality declaration is essential for the reliability of every system.

5. *The maintenance axis.* The availability of current data is of strategic importance for a land information system. Even the best system will soon deteriorate without proper maintenance of the information. From one viewpoint this axis can be included under point 4. as the age of data is

part of their quality. But because maintenance is such an important question, it is here treated as a separate point. No matter how strong the desire to simplify a cadastral/land registration system, a functioning method of maintenance *must* be included. However, a complete maintenance system need not be achieved all at once.

6. *The spatial axis.* Selectivity makes it possible to decide in detail which groups or which areas should be included in a certain system and also to differentiate methods. It is, therefore, one of the strongest means for adapting a project to existing resources.

As can be seen from these points and indeed from all the information presented in this study, cadastral/land registration systems have a high degree of cost flexibility, and can be implemented on very different levels. They can thus be adapted to various conditions. But as conditions and resources normally develop over time, it is of great importance that the system really is *progressive* irrespective of the level at which it begins. The system should be designed from the start in such a way that measures taken to extend and improve it do not mean sacrificing earlier work. The basic structure must be established with future needs in mind. How this can best be achieved in developed and developing countries should be a matter for serious thinking and research.

Summary

With the increasing complexity and problems of land planning and management, much attention has been devoted to the question of establishing better information systems as tools for improved land use and development. Parcel-based systems, especially cadastral/land registration systems, are an important component of such an information network. This study focuses on the problem of establishing or improving such systems. Therefore, it deals mainly with situations and countries in which adequate systems are lacking. This often means developing countries, but applies in some cases even to highly industrialized countries.

After the problem area is presented, the need for, and development of, land delimitation and documentation are discussed. Land demarcation and documentation should be regarded as a function of the general development of property rights. It is emphasized that improved specification of these rights is a means of stimulating intensified use and investment. Land documentation in maps and records can, therefore, be justified not only on the basis of its contribution to better public information, planning, valuation and management, but also because it gives greater security of tenure, improves production prerequisites and makes it easier to obtain investment credit. Some basic concepts in this connection such as parcel, cadastre and land registration are defined.

In Chapters 3–5 some main points are presented in the historical development of land records and cadastral and land registration models in Europe and in English speaking countries outside Europe. Some conclusions are drawn on the basis of this experience. Special consideration is given to the interplay between cadastres and land registers, and to the gradual establishment of some comprehensive, countrywide, multipurpose systems with a high degree of security.

The benefits of cadastres and land registers are treated in more detail in Chapters 6 and 7. Special emphasis is placed on their importance as a source of information for planning and administration, for the specification of rights and security of tenure, for credit provision, for the implementation of policy measures and for planning and regulating land use. In addition, cadastres and land registers provide a firmer basis for land assessment and taxation, facilitate transactions in land, stimulate a land market, reduce litigation in land and simplify the work of the courts. Most of these benefits are difficult to express in monetary terms. However, before introducing a new system, it is important to make *some* comparisons between benefits and costs. Certain comments are made on this problem.

Technical and administrative methods for establishing or improving cadastral/land registration systems are treated in Chapters 8–11. The importance of conducting a thorough feasibility study is emphasized. Such a study should include a background presentation, problem and benefit analysis, pilot studies, discussion of goals and methods, principles for phasing in and the legal measures needed to implement the programme. The main components in the introduction and maintenance of a system – cadastral surveying and demarcation, adjudication and registration – are treated with the special consideration given to the advantages of systematic operations, resulting in comprehensive, multipurpose records. It is presumed that the methods must usually be kept simple as those countries which lack adequate systems are often countries with meagre resources.

In Chapter 12 some specific problems are discussed. In many developing countries, long-term rights to land are held by a group – tribe, village, family, etc. – while individual rights are often temporary. In such cases the registration of group rights may be more appropriate. Even when the individual rights are stronger, group registration may still be considered as a first step to keep the initial costs low. Some viewpoints are presented on the problem of whether the consolidation of land should precede registration in cases of extreme fragmentation. Another problem concerns squatter rights, which will often be questioned when systematic registration is being carried out. On the one hand, few unregulated rights should remain after the operation has been completed. On the other hand, not all squatting units lacking formal rights are acceptable. The principles of systematic land registration must, therefore, be tempered by planning considerations, not least in urban areas.

Chapter 13 is devoted to questions of organization, automation and education. Land information and land management are the concerns of many different interests and authorities in a country. It is thus not possible for one single agency to develop and maintain cadastral/land registration systems. Links of co-operation and communication must be developed. This often involves the reorganization of old responsibilities and structures. Normally, one authority would be made chiefly responsible for developing and maintaining the system and acting as a spearhead for the whole project, and the collection of data would be handled by a number of agencies.

Automation is generally a central issue in the development of new systems, and this is also true in the case of cadastres and land registers. It is questionable whether automation should always be introduced from the start, but it must certainly be planned for in the long term. Some examples of solutions in different countries are presented. In the long run, databases will contain not only records of land units but also boundary co-ordinates and other information suitable for inclusion in a parcel-based system. The data will form a land information system not because they are combined in one single record or managed by one authority, but because they use the same identification keys, especially the land unit number.

Training and education must also be given great weight. International courses on the subject should be used, and national training programmes should be established – both short courses and university-level majors. 'On the job' training is essential as is more general information to administrators, landowners and the public. Since training and education take time, a programme should be developed from the very start of a new cadastre and land register project.

The analyses in this study deal mainly with the problems and methods of establishing comprehensive, multipurpose cadastral/land registration systems. However, when available resources are much too inadequate or when public opinion is not ripe, it may be necessary to start with other and cheaper alternatives. Chapter 14 is devoted to this discussion.

A fundamental first step is to divide the land into uniquely numbered units. A way of simplifying this operation is to start with large block units, which may be subdivided into smaller individual units at a later stage. The units should preferably be defined on index maps, which may be established by compiling existing survey materials or by conducting simple new surveys often based on photo-interpretation. Demarcation of boundaries can be simplified or even omitted in the first stage. Rights in land, which are determined provisionally in a simplified manner, may automatically gain legal force after a prescribed number of years if unchallenged. Another way to reduce costs is by exercising great selectivity in choosing areas to be included.

While the above-mentioned methods make it possible to introduce low-cost cadastral/land registration systems, it is important that their design facilitates future upgrading. This is the concept of 'progressive cadastre'.

The structure of the total study can be illustrated as shown in Fig. S.1.

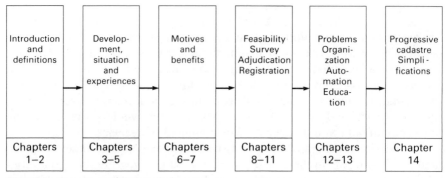

Fig. S.1 Structure of the study in summary

Appendix A

Land unit identifier

It is essential that every unit in a land unit reference system be uniquely identifiable. This is of special importance in a parcel-based land information system where the land unit identifier is the common key, linking different land databases.

The simplest identifier is a unit designation, which reflects the sequential order of registration in a countrywide or provincial system. This type of identifier has often been used when introducing registration – for example in connection with land grants in the former colonies – and it is still in use in many developing countries such as Zambia and Mozambique. However, this kind of designation does not give any indication of location, and it becomes impractical with increasing numbers of units and subdivisions. The same can be said about a grantor/grantee index, which identifies the unit by the names of the vendor and of the purchaser. It is widely used, especially in the USA and some parts of Canada, but it does not give a unique long-term definition of a parcel. Therefore, other methods are applied in most countries.

Dale and McLaughlin (1988, p. 41) present a list of desirable features in a reference system. It should be:

- easy to understand;
- easy to remember for the landowner;
- easy to use by the public and administrators;
- permanent, not requiring change in case of sale, etc.;
- capable of being updated at subdivision or amalgamation;
- unique and with perfect correspondence between record and ground;
- accurate and unlikely to be transcribed in error;

- flexible enough to be used in all forms of land administration;
- economical to introduce and to maintain.

Many types of identifiers have been used or discussed (see Ziemann 1976; Dale and McLaughlin *op. cit*). The following are the most important:

1. Hierarchical identification systems
    (a) *Volume and folio.*   Vol.45 Fol.175 means that the unit is described on the 175th page of the 45th volume, which normally also indicates the sequential order within the registration district of the first registration of the unit. It is a simple system, but apart from the fact that the location in a registration district is provided, it retains many of the drawbacks of a system based strictly on the order of registration.

    (b) *Plan number and unit number.*   This is often a number of the survey plan according to the date of the survey, with the land units numbered in some consecutive order within the plan. An alternative is to use the number of each topographical map-sheet, and to assign numbers to the units within a sheet in a certain order (according to time of registration or according to geographical position).

    (c) *Municipal unit – block – sub-block – land unit number.*   A municipal unit such as a county, city, town, township or municipality is subdivided into blocks and sub-blocks, within which land units are numbered in some consecutive order. The divisions are often based on existing sub-units such as town blocks or on administrative–historical boundaries such as those of a parish or village. The parish or village name can be used as a designation, but is often replaced by serial numbers, especially in connection with data processing. A unit may, for example, have the number 12–08–15–045, meaning unit no. 45 within village no. 15 within parish no. 8 within municipality no. 12, while on a daily basis, only the village name and unit number are used.

    (d) *Municipality and street address.*   A serial number can be substituted for the name of the street. The street address is probably the most widely understood of all identifiers, but not all land units are located alongside a road or have any natural link to a road. Neither are streets and roads always permanent. However, the street address is often used parallel with other land-unit designations.

2. Grid identification systems
    A grid is a set of mutually perpendicular and horizontal lines forming equal squares on a map, used as a reference for locating points and areas. Grid co-ordinates are a pair of numbers which locate a point in terms of its distance from two given axes (Ziemann).
    The grid may be related to latitude and longitude. Normally, however,

a co-ordinate system based on some kind of map projection is used – a national grid mapping system. Such co-ordinates of the boundary points will locate the land unit. If co-ordinates are to be used as land unit identifiers, however, *one* point must be chosen. Normally the approximate centrum point is used. This is an example of a *geocode*. Another example could be the co-ordinates for the main building. In other cases, for example when calculating traffic flows or travel distances, the distance to a point on a certain road section may be of interest. Examples of different geocodes are presented in Fig. A.1.

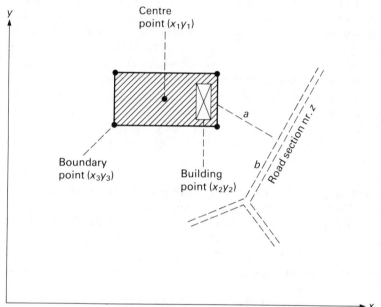

Fig. A.1   Examples of different geocodes

Grid co-ordinates or geocodes are very useful for locating parcel-based information in an automated system, and they are included with increasing frequence often in land unit records. However, they are rather impractical as identifiers because of their many digits which make them awkward for the general user. An improvement can be obtained by using *blocked* co-ordinates. For example, if the co-ordinates are 1234/5678, one could present them as 15/26/37/48 by pairing numerals in corresponding positions. The first two digits would then represent a higher geographical block, the next two a lower one, etc. For most purposes, one could omit the 15/26 and refer only to 37/48 (Ziemann).

3. Hybrid hierarchial/grid identifiers
   It may also be possible to use hybrid hierarchical/grid identifiers. For example, the province and the county could be identified by name or

number, while further identification of the land unit could follow a grid method. The *Rectangular Land Survey System*, which is predominant in the midwestern and western parts of the USA and Canada, is a hierarchical system, which consists of a basic grid in each of several survey areas, usually covering one or more states. The area is divided into townships, each of six square miles, and subdivided into 36 sections, each of one square mile (640 acres). There are some variations in the size of sections due to the curvature of the earth, changes in slope and elevation, etc. The 36-square-mile townships are numbered in terms of 'townships' north or south of the origin (only north in Canada) and in 'ranges' east or west of the prime meridian (only west in Canada). Within a township, the 36 sections are numbered. In the USA, the numbering starts in the upper right-hand corner (northeast). Within each section, the four quarter-sections are designated northeast, northwest, etc., and the quarter-quarter-sections are similarly designated. The northeast quarter of the southwest quarter of section 1, township 8 north, range 3 east of the fourth principal meridian is, for example, the specific identifier and locator for a 40-acre parcel in Dane County, Wisconsin (Fischer and Moyer 1973). This system provides the geographical location, but may be impractical in cases of successive subdivision, for example in an urban area.

Taking into consideration the advantages and disadvantages of different systems, Ziemann recommends a hierarchical identifier consisting of the elements (state)–county–tract–group–source parcel–affix. The source parcel is here the original land unit, while affix is the number given at subdivision. With this method, the source parcel number can be retained even after subdivision or other changes. County–tract–group can be designated by number or by names.

Ziemann continues: 'Within the source parcel number system several affix solutions are possible: numerical or alphabetical affix, single or multiple affix. Numerals are more convenient than alphabetical characters and are therefore recommended. Multiple affixes would create additional digits with each boundary change and could therefore soon become very long. Hence, a single affix is suggested.'

In Sweden, for example, a hierarchical system is used, starting with the name of the municipality and normally continuing with the name of the village or town. In the designation Alby 5:18 in the municipality of Botkyrka, Botkyrka is the municipality, Alby the village, 5 one of the original farms in the village, while the affix 18 is determined by later partitions and subdivisions.

Appendix B

Two examples of automation: Sweden and Canada

The Swedish Land Data Bank System

The description of the system – the principles of which were worked out by a project team led by Helmer Wallner – is compiled from information material published by the Central Board for Real Estate Data.

All Sweden is subdivided in real estate units – about 4 million in total. The units are described in a cadastre – a real property register with relevant maps and other documentation. The original survey maps are normally in the scale 1:1000–1:4000 in rural areas and 1:400–1:1000 in urban areas. These maps have been compiled to register index maps in standard sheets – in the rural areas mostly by combining existing map material, photo-interpretation and field checks and establishment of a comprehensive map in the scale 1:10000. Property registration is made on a county or city level, but the National Land Survey has a supervisory responsibility.

The legal rights to the unit are registered in land registers by Land Register Agencies. These are part of the lower courts and are administratively supervised by the National Court Administration. The registers are of the title type.

For about 20 years the handling of real property and land registration has been in the process of being automated. An EDP system is replacing the earlier register books. The system is now operational in most of Sweden and will be completed about 1995. A governmental agency – the Central Board for Real Estate Data (CFD) – has the main responsibility for development, implementation and processing of the system. The work is carried out in close co-operation with the land survey and the court organizations.

The Land Data Bank System is an on-line system built up around a central computer. The primary users – the Real Property Register and Land Register

Agencies – use display terminals and printers connected to the computer via leased telephone lines. Information retrieval from display terminals is possible for banks, municipalities, survey agencies, brokers, insurance companies and other major users of land information. (see Fig. B.1).

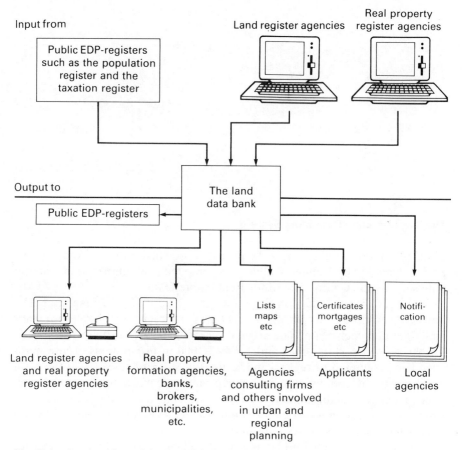

Fig. B.1 An overview of the Swedish Land Data Bank System

Only the Real Property Register and the Land Register Agencies are permitted to update the register contents and they are only permitted to change data concerning their own jurisdiction. Information retrieval is not limited in this way; each display terminal has access to any part of the system.

Formally, the contents of the Land Data Bank System are divided into a real property register and a land register. The contents can be seen in Fig. B.2. Information retrieved by means of local terminals can be presented either on a display terminal screen, on a printer or on both. Official documents like title deeds, mortgage bonds and certain register extracts are printed out at the central computer and distributed therefrom directly to the applicants. Examples of register extracts are:

- certificate of real property, containing all the information that the Land Data Bank System possesses on property units;

- certificate of search, containing information such as area, rights, assessed value, owner, mortgages;

- certificate of plans, with details pertaining to a plan.

Also thematic maps on population and housing, for example, are produced as a result of communication possibilities between the Land Data Bank System and other data sources.

With the system efficient and reliable title registration is facilitated. The general course of an automated land registration process is shown in Fig. B.3. Another main responsibility is to provide information for land management and urban and regional planning. This task is mainly based on the registration of co-ordinates and the linking of the system with other public EDP registers. Co-ordinates are captured by digitizing. They are recorded for the central point of the land unit, for main buildings and for historical monuments. The national co-ordinate system is used. With the help of the co-ordinate method can statistics be presented for 'functional areas' instead of only for administrative areas. Data lists and statistical tables can be replaced by a graphical presentation in the form of maps. Joint processing of the co-ordinates in the Land Data Bank System and data from public EDP systems means the data can be presented as grid maps, dot maps or isarithmic maps (see, for example, Fig. B.4).

The linking with other systems is mainly based on the fact that

- the same land unit designation is used as identifier not only in the Land Data Bank System but also in other systems;

- there is in the population register information on the property unit on which each person lives;

- the civic registration number for each person is widely used as identifier in public EDP systems.

This makes it possible to easily get lists not only of all land units within an arbitrary area, but also all property owners as well as persons with other characteristics such as a certain age, sex, profession, etc.

The LRIS system in the Maritime Provinces of Canada

Information sources are mainly Simpson (1984) and Dale and McLaughlin (1988).

For each real property unit the land data bank system contains mainly the following information:

Location
The administrative area where the real property unit is located, the address, its location on the real property register map, centroid coordinates for the unit and coordinates for the buildings situated on the property.

Area
The area of the real property unit.

Value
The tax assessment value.

Owner
The name, address and civic registration number of the owner/owners, particulars on how (for example by purchase) and when the real property unit was acquired. The purchasing sum is also shown.

Plans and regulations
Building plans and regulations affecting the unit.

Encumbrances
Mortgages: The amount of the mortgages and the name of the holder of the mortgage bond.
Easements: For example obligation to allow the owner of another real property unit to make use of a facility situated on the unit.

Entitlements
Easements that are beneficial for the real property unit, for example the right to use a private road.

Survey measures
Formal and technical measures that have been taken, a document identification number referring to maps and other documents in archives is shown.

Notations
For example notations on executional measures.

Fig. B.2   The contents of the Swedish Land Data Bank System

The Land Registration and Information Service (LRIS) programme was a comprehensive attempt to resolve a set of problems related to land information management in the Maritimes, such as:

- a land registry system that still indexed interests in land parcels according to the names of parties to each transaction, not by the parcel itself;

- no co-ordinated approach to link land data collected and maintained by different land management agencies;

- no medium-scale base mapping suitable for multiple uses;

- urban base mapping done by municipalities who could afford it;

- no second-order control survey system.

The LRIS programme has consisted of four phases:

An illustration of how a registration of title is handled in the Land Data Bank System. The turn-around time is 3–4 days.

Client

The applicant has bought a real property unit and has to apply for registration of title to it within three months. The application form and the documents required are sent to the Land Register Agency.

The applicant receives the results of this application after 3–4 days. On receipt he has to pay stamp duty and a charge.

Computer Centre

As a result of the decision made by the land register agency the applicant will receive a certificate. This certificate and all other documents are printed out at the computer centre after the updating. Next day the documents are mailed directly to the applicant.

At the computer centre information is stored on disks. All instructions from the register agencies regarding amendments to register contents are stored in an intermediate database. After office hours the contents of the intermediate database are used to steer updating of the registers. This is carried out by batch processing.

Printer

Disk storage

Computer

Land Register Agency

Everyday work with land registration is carried out in on-line processing as a dialogue between the operator and the computer.

The operator enters on the display screen what kind of job is to be processed in this case an application for registration of title in connection with the purchase of a real property unit. The civic registration numbers of both seller and buyer, the real property unit's designation, the buyer's name and the purchasing sum are stated and a decision is proposed.

From the display terminal the various details are sent one by one to the computer. Every time a message is received the computer executes a number of checkroutines – for example that the seller is the owner of the real property unit. Errors are immediately indicated on the screen and processing is halted until the error is corrected.

On the screen are also shown other messages of significance for the process, for example that the seller is married and therefore needs the spouse's consent for the sale, that the municipality has the first option, or that an acquisition licence from the County Agricultural Board is required. The administration fee and stamp duty are calculated by the computer.

When processing is completed, a message is sent to the computer, which in return confirms that no further measures are required. On the screen is shown the diary number for this particular job. A separate diary-sheet is automatically printed out on a printer connected to the display terminal. The diary-sheet can be used to check that the job has been handled correctly.

Usually once a day, jobs that have been processed are confirmed. This is done from the display terminal by using a personal password.

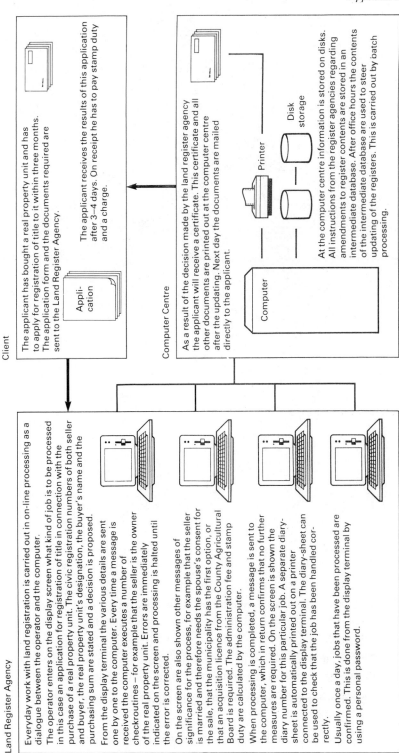

Fig. B.3 The land registration process in the Swedish system

Fig. B.4 Number of children, aged 4–6 years, within a radius of 400 m (used for school planning)

1. The establishment and maintenance of a second-order control survey system.

2. The production and maintenance of base maps and property maps to serve resource management, urban development and parcel identification needs.

3. The gradual replacement of the existing rudimentary deed registry system in each province with a computer-based land titles system.

4. The creation of a series of integrated land records.

The control programme (phase 1) is now in a maintenance mode, while the initial programme of large-scale mapping for all urban areas and the coverage of the entire land mass with medium-scale maps was completed in 1984. The production of a new digital map is on going. Cadastral maps and computer files have been created for more than 750 000 parcels. As new areas are covered by property mapping, the task of updating property maps and associated parcel data files grows. LRIS policy is to maintain the parcel information concurrently with the plans and transactions filed at land registry office.

Land titles legislation has been passed and a demonstration project has been commenced in one of the provinces – New Brunswick. It appears that the province is going to support a comprehensive title conversion programme.

Concerning the fourth phase it was initially envisaged that the service would create and maintain a large, centralized land data bank. This concept has, however, not been accepted. Many government agencies and private organizations have established their own computer-based data files. Efforts have shifted to the development of distributed land information networks, in which each organization will maintain responsibility for its own data.

While some parts of the programme, such as the implementation and maintenance of the control network, have had difficulty in obtaining funds; other parts such as the cadastral mapping programme have met widespread political support. Phase 3 has been deemed to give acceptable gains, too. In principle also the benefits of integrating land records have been universally accepted. Recently LRIS has been replaced by another type of organization, but the activities will certainly continue.

References and bibliography

Acquaye, E. and **Crocombe, R.** (eds.) (1984) *Land Tenure and Rural Productivity in the Pacific Islands.* FAO, Rome.

Acquaye, E. and **Murphy, M. C.** (1973) *Land Use, Land Tenure and Agricultural Development in Ghana.* FAO, Rome.

Allot, A. (1971) Theoretical and practical limitations to registration of title in tropical Africa. Seminar on problems of land tenure in African development. Afrika-Studiecentrum, Leiden.

Andersson, S. (1980) Swedish land information systems. *The Canadian Surveyor*, **34** (1).

Angus-Leppan, P. (1983) Economic costs and benefits of land information. FIG Congress, Sofia.

Badekas, J. (1981) Cadastre or data bank? A dilemma for countries under development. FIG Congress, Montreux.

Bernhardsen, T. and **Tveitdal, S.** (1987) Community benefit of digital spatial information. In: *Advanced Course in the Development of Cadastral Systems.* National Land Survey of Sweden, Gävle.

Bernstein, J. D. (1986) *The Costs of Land Information Systems.* The World Bank, Washington.

Blachut, T. J. and **Villasana, J. A.** (1974) *Cadastre. Various Functions, Characteristics, Techniques and the Planning of a Modern Land Records System.* National Research Council Canada, Ottawa.

Bogaerts, M. J. M. (1985) Improvements of cadastres and other land information systems in developing countries. Urban data management symposium, The Hague.

Boyes, W. S. (1971) Experience with cadastral survey systems in the developing islands of the Pacific. Commonwealth Survey Officers Conference, Cambridge.

Brahiti, A. (1981) Etablissement du cadastre et institution du livre foncier en Algérie. FIG Congress, Montreux.

Burrough, P. A. (1986) *Principles of Geographical Information Systems for Land Resources Assessment.* Clarendon Press, Oxford.

Chrisman, N. R. *et al.* (1986) Soil erosion planning in Wisconsin: an application and evaluation of a multi-purpose land information system. FIG Congress, Toronto.

Coker, C. B. A. (1958) *Family Property among the Yorubas.* London University Press, London.
Crocombe, R. (1964) *Land Tenure in the Cook Islands.* Oxford University Press, Melbourne.
Crocombe, R. (ed.) (1977) *Land Tenure in the Pacific.* Oxford University Press and University of the South Pacific, Suva.
Crocombe, R. (1984) *Registration in the Pacific Islands: Experiences and Potentials. Land Tenure and Rural Productivity in the Pacific Islands.* FAO, Rome.

Dale, P. F. (1976) *Cadastral Surveys within the Commonwealth.* HMSO, London.
Dale, P. F. (1983) Boundaries and Surveys. FIG Congress, Sofia.
Dale, P. F. and **McLaughlin, J. D.** (1988) *Land Information Management.* Clarendon Press, Oxford.
Demsetz, H. (1967) Toward a theory of property rights. *American Economic Review,* **57.**
Dobner, H. K. (1983) Mexico City's new integral cadastral information system. FIG Congress, Sofia.
Doebele, W. (1985) Why cadastral systems are important for less developed countries. *The Urban Edge,* **9.**
Domer, P. (1972) *Land Reform and Economic Development.* Penguin, London.
Dowson, E. and **Sheppard, V. L. O.** (1968) *Land registration,* 3rd edn. HMSO, London.
Dreux, T. (1933) *Le Cadastre et l'impôt foncier.* Paris.
Dueker, K. J., Clapp, J. L. and **Niemann, B. J.** (1986) North American land information system: An overview with recommendations, 1986. FIG Congress, Toronto.
Dunlop, K. C. (1983) Implementation and operation of the Cayman Island Land Registry. Commonwealth Survey Officers Conference, Cambridge.
Durussel, R. (1980) Constitution du cadastre numérique à l'aide des mesurations existantes, analyse et méthode. Ecole Polytechnique Fédérale de Lausanne. Thèse no. 371.

Eichhorn, G. (1980) Auf- und Ausbau von Landinformationssystemen in Industrie- und Entwicklungsländern. *Zeitschrift für Vermessungswesen,* no. 12.

Feder, G. (1986) The economic implications of land ownership security in rural Thailand. Paper prepared for the World Bank seminar on land information management, Annapolis, Md.
Feder, G. (1987) Land registration and titling from an economist's perspective: a case study in rural Thailand, *Survey Review,* **29.**
Féderation Internationale des Géomètres (FIG). Congress papers. Commissions 3 and 7. Congresses 1977 (Stockholm), 1981 (Montreux), 1983 (Sofia), 1986 (Toronto), 1990 (Helsinki).
Fischer, K. P. and **Moyer, D. D.** (1973) *Land Parcel Identifier for Land Information Systems.* Chicago Press.
Förstner, F. and **Hothmer, J.** (1971) Aerophotogrammetric maps for the establishment of cadastre in developing countries. FIG Congress, Wiesbaden.

Ganesan, S. (1975) Cadastral surveys in India. Commonwealth Survey Officers Conference, Cambridge.
Gonzales-Fletcher, A. (1980) Modern technology in cadastral operations in developing countries. *Canadian Surveyor,* **34** (1).
Greulich, G. (1983) Title insurance: A pre-cadastral necessity. FIG Congress, Sofia.

Hailey, Lord (1952) The land tenure problems in Africa. *Journal of African Administration*, special supplement.

Hamilton, A. C. and **McLaughlin, J. D.** (ed.) (1984) *The Decision Maker and Land Information Systems*. Canadian Institute of Surveying, Ottawa.

Hamilton A. C. and **Williamson. I. P.** (1984) A critique of the FIG definition of 'Land Information System'. *The Decision Maker and Land Information Systems*. Canadian Institute of Surveying, Ottawa.

Henssen, J. L. G. (1971) The principles of publicity and speciality in connection with the liaison between cadastre and land records. FIG Congress, Wiesbaden.

Henssen, J. L. G. (1975) Maintenance of cadastres. *World Cartography*, **XII**. United Nations.

Henssen, J. L. G. (1981) The requirements and significance of a land registration system, including the cadastre, for developing countries. FIG Congress, Montreux.

Henssen, J. L. G. (1987) Cadastral and land registration systems in Europe. In: *Advanced Course in the Development of Cadastral Systems*. National Land Survey of Sweden, Gävle.

Henssen, J. L. G. and **McLaughlin, J. D.** (1986) The development of a conceptual framework for the study of cadastral systems. FIG Congress, Toronto.

Henssen, J. L. G. and **Williamson, J. P.** (1990) Land registration, cadastre and its interaction. A world perspective. FIG Congress, Helsinki.

Hesse, W. and **Williamson, J. P.** (1990) Current status and future directions of digital cadastral data bases (DCDB) in Australia and New Zealand. FIG Congress, Helsinki.

Hoeflinger, E. (1986) Die Nutzung der österreichischen Gründstucksdaten bank mit dem medium Bildschirmtext. FIG Congress, Toronto.

Hoeflinger, E. (1990) Der Ausbau eines Landinformationssystems in Österreich. FIG Congress, Helsinki.

Holstein, L. C. (1987) Considerations for land registration improvement for less developed countries. *Survey Review*, **29**.

Howells, L. J. (1974) The cadastral survey and registration project in the Caribbean. *Chartered Surveyor*, supplement.

International Workshop on Land Tenure Administration (1984) *Proceedings*. Salvador, Brazil.

Janczyk, J. T. (1979) Land title systems, scale of operations, and operating and conversion costs. *The Journal of Legal Studies*, **VIII** (3).

Kennedy, W. D. (1983) Thailand land titling project. Commonwealth Survey Officers Conference, Cambridge.

Knetsch, J. and **Trebilcock, M.** (1981) *Land Policy and Economic Development in Papua New Guinea*. Institute of National Affairs, Port Moresby.

Kurandt, F. (1955) Grundsätzliches zur Aufstellung eines Liegenschaftskatasters. *Allg. Vermess. Nachr*. 1955:3.

Kurandt, F. (1957) *Grundbuch und Liegenschaftskataster*. Herbert Wickman Verlag, Berlin.

Larsson. G. (1971) Land registration in developing countries. *World Cartography*, **XI**. United Nations.

Larsson. G. (1977) The evolution of the existing cadastres towards the multipurpose cadastre. FIG Congress, Stockholm.

Larsson, G. and **Stoimenov, G.** (1985) *Needs and Methods of Systematic Land Information in Connection with the New Agricultural Policy of Tanzania*. Mimo, Stockholm.

Lawrance, J. C. D. (1970) The role of registration of title in the evolution of customary tenures and its effects on societes in Africa. Seminar of the UN Economic Commission for Africa. Addis Ababa.

Lawrance, J. C. D. (1984) *Overview. Land Tenure and Rural Productivity in the Pacific Islands.* FAO, Rome.

Lawrance, J. C. D. (1985) Land adjudication. Paper presented at World Bank seminar on land information systems.

Lawrance Mission (1966) *Report of the Mission on Land Consolidation and Registration in Kenya.* London.

Ley, A. (1981) L'Evolution du droit foncier ivorien depuis l'indépendence du 7 Août 1960. FIG Congress, Montreux.

Love, R. J. (1968) Land tenure in Australia. FIG Congress, London.

Lundgren, R. (1987) Aerial photography for production of registry maps. *Advanced Course in the Development of Cadastral Systems.* National Land Survey of Sweden, Gävle.

McLaughlin, J. D. (1983) Standards for multipurpose cadastral systems. FIG Congress, Sofia.

Matthias, H. J. (1990) Control networks, large scale mapping, legal surveys, cadastre, land property registration, land information systems around the world. An international inquiry in all FIG countries. FIG Congress, Helsinki.

Meek, C. K. (1946) *Land Law and Custom in the Colonies.* Oxford University Press.

Megary, R. E. and **Wade, H. W. R.** (1959) *The Law of Real Property.* 2nd edn. London.

Mifsud, F. M. (1967) *Customary Land Law in Africa.* FAO, Rome.

Morgan, G. (1985) Land information systems. Design considerations for the organisation of supporting technologies. *The Urban Edge,* **9**.

National Research Council Panel on a Multipurpose Cadadastre (1980, 1982) *Need for a Multipurpose Cadastre. Procedures and standards for a multipurpose cadastre.* National Academy Press, Washington, DC.

Nittinger, J. (1974) Cadastral surveying as an instrument of political, economic and social development. Seminar of cadastral surveying and urban mapping. German Foundation for International Development, Berlin.

Ollennu, N. A. (1962) *Customary Land Law in Ghana.* London.

Onsrud, H. (1984) GAB: a land information system of benefit to the public as well as to the private sector. *The Decision Maker and Land Information Systems.* Canadian Institute of Surveying, Ottawa.

Pasteur, D. (1979) *The Management of Squatter Upgrading.* Saxon House, Farnborough.

Petrov, E. (1983) Cadastre des propriétés foncières rurales en RP de Bulgarie. FIG Congress, Sofia.

Rhodes, M. L. and **Crane, E.** (1984) Lands – a multipurpose land information system. In: *The Decision Maker and Land Information Systems.* Canadian Institute of Surveying, Ottawa.

Robertson, W. A. (1990) An operational multipurpose cadastre and beyond: the New Zealand experience. FIG Congress, Helsinki.

Ruoff, R. B. (1968) English registered title to land and the function of ordnance survey maps. FIG Congress, London.

Saussol, A. (1979) *L'Héritage: Essai sur le Problème Foncier Mélanésian en Nouvelle Calédonie.* Société des Océanistes, no. 40. Paris.

Schenk, E. (1990) Das Liegenschaftskataster in der Bundesrepublik Deutschland – Stand und weitere Entwicklung. FIG Congress, Helsinki.

Scott, R. (1981) The multipurpose land information system in the public sector community of the North American continent. FIG Congress, Montreux.

Sedunary, M. E. (1984) LOTS, and the Nodal Approach to a Total Land Information System. *The Decision Maker and Land Information System.* Canadian Institute of Surveying, Ottawa.

Simmerding, F. (1974) Establishment of a cadastre. Seminar of cadastral surveying and urban mapping. German Foundation for International Development, Berlin.

Simpson, A. W. B. (1961) *An Introduction to the History of the Land Law.* Oxford University Press.

Simpson, R. L. (1984) LRIS – The basis for land information systems. In: *The Decision Maker and Land Information System.* Canadian Institute of Surveying, Ottawa.

Simpson, S. R. (1967) The role of maps and boundaries in land registration. Commonwealth Survey Officers Conference, Cambridge.

Simpson, S. R. (1976) *Land Law and Registration.* Cambridge University Press.

Smith, P. J. (1990) The place of H.M. Land Registry in the development of a national geographic information system in the U.K. FIG Congress, Helsinki.

Sorrenson, M. P. K. (1967) *Land Reform in the Kikuye County.* Oxford University Press, Nairobi.

Stubkjaer, E. (1981) *Land Use Control and Property Registration in the Nordic Countries.* Aalborg University Press.

Swank, R. (1983) Geographic data system in Lane County. Ten years of development. FIG Congress, Sofia.

Ternryd, C. O. (1975) The real estate data bank in Sweden and the connections to other data banks. Commonwealth Survey Officers Conference, Cambridge.

Turner, J. F. C. (1976) *Housing by People.* Marion Boyars, London.

United Nations (1973) *Report of the Ad Hoc Group of Experts on Cadastral Surveying and Mapping.* New York.

United Nations (1985) *Report of the Ad Hoc Group of Experts on Cadastral Surveying and Land Information Systems.* New York.

Wallner, H. (1969) The cadastre as the basis of an environmental data system. *The Canadian Surveyor,* June.

Watson, H. R. (1971) Cadastral surveys in West Indian Islands. Commonwealth Survey Officers Conference, Cambridge.

Weir, C. H. (1984) Introduction. *The Decision Maker and Land Information Systems.* Canadian Institute of Surveying, Ottawa.

West, H. W. (1969) The role of land registration in developing countries. *Chartered Surveyor.* November.

White, C. A. (1983) *A History of the Rectangular Survey System.* Government Printing Office, Washington DC.

Williamson, I. P. (1983) Cadastral survey techniques in developing countries – with particular reference to Thailand. *The Australian Surveyor,* **31** (7).

Williamson, I. P. (1986) Cadastral and land information systems – where are we heading? Sixth Australian Cartographic Conference, Melbourne.

Ziemann, H. (1976) *Land Unit Identification.* An Analysis. National Research Council of Canada, Ottawa.

Index